Pippa's Challenge

Lately Pippa had behaved rather aloofly, and reduced our time together strictly to her feeding hours. She had always shown her affection by brushing herself against me, nibbling my hand in playful way, purring and looking with soft eyes at me when she was happy. Now there were many people around and we were never left alone.

I was painfully aware that our intimate relationship had been injured, so I arranged to follow the family and remain with Pippa for as long as it might take to restore it. It was touching to see how quickly Pippa reacted. After I had caressed her, she put her head close to mine and purred. I knew that I was again accepted into her world.

Pippa's Challenge

Joy Adamson

Fontana/Collins

First published by Wm. Collins and The Harvill Press 1972
First issued in Fontana Books 1973

Printed in Great Britain
Collins Clear-Type Press
London and Glasgow

*To all who love cheetah and help these
magnificent animals to survive*

Contents

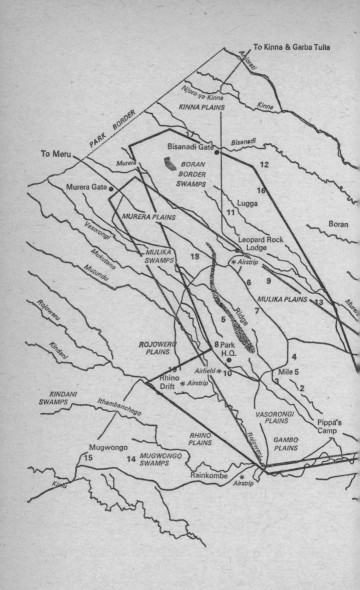

1 Pippa's mating place for fourth litter

2 Birthplace of fourth litter

3 Male cub killed by lion

4 Hans Lugga

5 Lava Plateau

6 Golo rendezvous

7 'Feeding Acacia' where cubs chased rhino

8 Cubs found after 46 days, and Boy found injured

9 First mating of cubs

10 Airstrip at Headquarters

11 'Feeding Terminalia' in Boran country

12 The cubs last seen – Boran country

13 Pippa and cubs killed Grevy

14 George's camp at Mugwongo

15 Whity and Tatu seen

16 Whity seen on last day in Meru – October 1970

17 Whity photographed by Mpanga

18 Tatu seen injured with 2 cubs

19 Whity photographed by George

———————— Territory of the fourth litter

———————— Territory of Mbili, Whity and Tatu

The author would like to express her gratitude to Dr N. Tinbergen, *Science* and U.P.I. for permission to quote Mr Joseph L. Myler's article 'Is Brain Mankind's Enemy?', published in the *Savannah Morning News*, 8 September 1968, in which Mr Myler used extracts from 'On War and Peace in Animals and Man' by Dr N. Tinbergen, published in *Science*, 28 June 1968.

She would also like to thank The Zoological Society of London for permission to quote Mr V. J. A. Manton's article 'Breeding cheetahs (*Acinonyx jubatus*) at Whipsnade Park', published in the International Zoo Yearbook, 1970.

Illustrations

Section 3

Love play would start gently with clasping, or with
  a mock fight
'Jetting'
Mating . . . and the final neck bite
Resting under a bush
Often all three cubs would flirt . . . and mate
Love play would continue
Licking noses and tongues
An ambush
Mating

Foreword

Since the publication of *The Spotted Sphinx*, I have often been asked what I regard as my most significant insight into cheetah behaviour. All I have learned during the four and a half years I shared Pippa's life in the Meru National Park could be briefly described in two major sections: Birth Control and Telepathy.

We know that cheetah have a gestation of 100-103 days and that they come into oestrus (season) every few weeks (the exact period I have not yet been able to find out). I learned from Pippa that she will not mate while she is rearing her litters, she waits until the cubs are independent of her help, which happens at about fifteen months. During this time I have never seen her in the company of a male, although on a few occasions I traced the spoor of a male not far from the family.

The cubs started eating meat when five weeks old, but carried on suckling until they were eleven weeks and five days old; at least, it was at this age that I saw Big Boy suckling, but Pippa still had a little milk when the cubs were twenty-four weeks and five days old.

Tragically, she lost two of her four litters to predators: the first within six weeks, and the third when the cubs were thirteen days old, at which time she had hardly recovered from giving birth, yet she mated and conceived within a week. After losing her first litter, she mated within three weeks. This shows that on both occasions she must have known that her unfortunate young were dead and no longer needed her. This knowledge seemed to have released a 'psychological block' which otherwise would have eliminated her sexual desires during the period in which she was occupied in rearing her cubs. It also proves that cheetah are 'inducive ovulators' who, stimulated by the presence of a male, can get into oestrus even if they have hardly recovered from giving birth and are still fully lactating. If we could find out more about the co-ordination of psychology and the physical organs (and in particular, the reproductive organs) of cheetah females and lionesses, both of which behave in the same way, it might be of great value to human beings in controlling the disastrous population problem, for all mammals have basically the same reproductive organs.

I was not only fascinated to see how Pippa could ovulate instantly after she had lost her young, but also to discover how she knew where to find a mate. In *The Spotted Sphinx* I have already described how she lost no time in mating once she knew that her cubs could kill (this was at fourteen months, although at this age they still needed her help for a few more weeks to gain sufficient practice).

While she went off to find a mate she seemed to have 'ordered' her cubs, Whity and Tatu – to remain within two miles of my camp, and I assumed she did this knowing that I would help feed them during her absence. Whity and Tatu hardly moved while their mother was absent. I visited them every day and they accepted my food, but their growls made it very plain that I was only tolerated for this reason. Meanwhile I traced Pippa's spoor running in an almost straight line for eight miles till she evidently found a male. How did she know he was there?

After a week she reappeared in camp, refused the food I offered her, and went off in a great hurry to her waiting cubs. I followed her with the meat; only after they were reunited did Pippa gulp it down so greedily that I could judge how hungry she had been.

During Pippa's absence her third cub, Mbili, had been away on her own for seventeen days. Although I was very worried and searched daily for her, Pippa seemed unconcerned, it was as if she knew that Mbili was safe, and in fact she returned in perfect condition. Yet on the occasions when we had removed Whity and Dume from the family, to cure them of their leg injuries, Pippa had searched desperately for many days for them and was very subdued.

Before finally breaking the ties with her children Pippa introduced them to their future hunting-grounds, each neighbouring the other and large enough to provide enough food. By some obscure law none of the cubs, either at the start or later on, ever trespassed on each other's territory, though they often met along their borders, nor did they ever follow Pippa back into camp. This seemed to indicate that female cheetah have stricter territorial instincts than the males, who move around more casually even when both sexes use 'scent-markings' to warn intruders off.

All this might suggest that Pippa could communicate not only with her cubs, but also with her mate, over distances so great that neither sound nor scent could help her; the only answer seems to be that she communicated by telepathy. Moreover, the instances described in *The Spotted Sphinx*, in which Guitus' 'heart' would guide him to the cheetah family – and Pippa had especially reacted to his 'heart' by retracing her way to meet us – seem to indicate that human beings who live as close to nature, as this ranger had done all his life, retain their power of thought communication to a far stronger extent than more sophisticated people. This bears out my belief that man originally possessed the power of telepathy to the same degree that wild animals seem to have retained it, but that when he developed speech, and later mechanical means of communication (such as radio, print, cables) the glands responsible for thought communication became atrophied. Certainly today only a few people can count, in a rather unreliable way, on their powers of telepathy. For the last thirty years I, too, have lived a life close to nature in Kenya, and have, in consequence, developed an acute extra-sensory perception in relation to animals. For instance, although both were far away from me at the time, I knew the moment Elsa and

Dume had died. With my own kind this extra-sensory perception works to a lesser degree.

Another instance which seemed to suggest telepathy was the time described in *The Spotted Sphinx* when Pippa appeared to know that George's assistant would bring her fresh meat. None of us were aware that he was out to get a kill, but she sat expectantly for hours on the road until he turned up late in the afternoon, with a carcass for her. Elsa behaved in the same way on the occasion when I took her sisters to Nairobi to be flown to Holland. George remained with her at our home 200 miles away and had no idea when I would return. But Elsa *knew* and waited all day at the entrance drive, watching the direction from which I eventually arrived.

In the 'Elsa' books I also mention other instances which can only be explained by telepathy. For example, Elsa knew when we decided to visit her at her camp, was always waiting for us when we arrived after our 180 mile drive and later, when we traced her fresh spoor, invariably we found that she had covered great distances to come to meet us. Again, she often controlled her cubs causing them to remain immobile in our care, while, in dangerous fights, she defended her territory from the 'fierce lioness' who had been its former owner. If the cubs were missing I worried, but Elsa seemed to know that they were safe.

Both Elsa's and Pippa's telepathic sense appeared to be reliable so far as direct communication between them and their young, or them and me, was concerned.

Medical research suggests that it is the pineal and pituitary glands, as well as the hyperthalamus, which are responsible for sexual development and that they may also be responsible for thought communication. But up to date we know little of the functions and co-ordination of these glands. If we were to learn more about thought communication from the behaviour of these wild cats, and if afterwards we could analyse the function of these glands, we might learn something of immense importance and which would lead us towards a better understanding of some aspects of life that we desperately need to understand if we want to survive. The over-specialization of our intellect has separated us dangerously from all the other creatures around us, and unless we find a way of becoming again a constructive part of the 'balance of nature', we may not only disappear, as have other species which became over-specialized and outlived their environment, but we may also take everything alive with us. Although we are the most evolved and intellectually advanced of all animals, we are certainly the most destructive.

In an article from the *Savannah Morning News* of the 8th of September 1968, entitled 'Is Brain Mankind's Enemy?', Joseph L. Myler (UPI Senior Editor, Washington UPI) wrote: 'The "frightening and ironical" thought that the human brain may be mankind's worst enemy is suggested by Dr N. Tinbergen, Professor of Animal Behaviour in the Department of Zoology at Oxford University.

'Man, Tinbergen points out,* is the only animal which commits mass murder against members of its own species.

'Because of his marvellous brain, the professor notes, man has evolved culturally far faster than he has genetically. Genetically, he is not much different from the prehistoric man who painted the caves of southern France. "But culturally, we have changed beyond recognition, and are changing at an ever-increasing rate." Man's brain has enabled him to achieve "a mastery of our environment that is without precedent in the history of life". It has enabled him to "rape" the earth, pollute air and water and soil, to bring about a population explosion threatening whole peoples with death by starvation, and to create long-range weapons of mass destruction which could close the book on civilization.

'The human brain, apparently, is a sort of Jekyll-Hyde organ. Tinbergen, in a discussion of the subject in the technical weekly *Science*, writes that there is a part of it which has made it possible for man to develop a life of reason. But there is another

* 'On War and Peace in Animals and Man', N. Tinbergen, *Science*, Vol. 160, p. 160, pp. 1411-1418, 28 June 1968. Copyright © 1968 by the American Association for the Advancement of Science.

part of his brain which binds man to the "instincts" of his animal heritage, and limits his ability to change his behaviour as rapidly as he changes his environment and his tools for war or peace. According to Tinbergen "we are still, to ourselves, unknown". We lack understanding of the causes and effects of the function of our brains.

'He believes that a "scientific knowledge of our behaviour, leading to its control, may well be the most urgent task that faces mankind today. It is the effects of our behaviour that begin to endanger the very survival of our species and, worse, of all life on earth . . . the human brain, the finest life-preserving device created by evolution, has made our species so successful in mastering the outside world that it suddenly finds itself taken off guard. One could say that our cortex and our brainstem (our 'reason' and our 'instincts') are at loggerheads. Together they have created a new social environment in which, rather than ensuring our survival, they are about to do the opposite."

'It is the job of science "to understand this enemy", one way to attempt this is through studying animal behaviour. This may not show how to eliminate aggressive conduct, but it might disclose ways of "taking the sting out of it". Only man is an "uninhibited killer".'

Since Pippa offered unique opportunities for learning more about wild cheetah behaviour the National Park Authorities agreed that I should continue my studies for another eighteen months, until her fourth litter would be independent. Like this, I would not only be able to compare their developments with that of her former cubs, and discover if what I had learned up to now was the norm of cheetah behaviour, but I might hope to find out what would happen should Pippa meet her previous cubs, alone, or with their offspring while her fourth litter was still dependent on her. Finally, I might have a chance to see how she would decide on territorial rights for her increasing family and how they would select their mates. Nobody had ever seen a wild cheetah mating, or knew when they began puberty.

1. The Fourth Litter

Now Pippa was close to her hour for the fourth time and I had recently watched her movements anxiously. For the last four days she had been missing and so I was very glad to see her walking into camp at teatime on the 13th of July 1968. She came from the nearby plain where she had given birth to her last litter and where, when thirteen days old, these unfortunate cubs were killed by a hyena. Since then the vegetation in the area had grown into a thick scrub and had become more of a trap to animals of Pippa's size than a suitable nursery. I was therefore surprised that she had frequented this place during the last weeks, and that she headed back to it again as soon as she had eaten a hearty meal.

Local and I followed her for half a mile, after which she sat down and would not budge. While I patted her and felt her milk-swollen nipples she rolled over; at that moment I saw four elephants approaching us swiftly. There was nothing left for us to do but to run. Glancing back I saw the giants steadily advance towards Pippa who, as on many other occasions, ignored them. Today this puzzled me, as her condition indicated that she would give birth within the next forty-eight hours.

We had watched these elephants hanging round the camp for the last five days and all our efforts to chase them away had not stopped them from browsing persistently at a few trees close to our huts, as though these were the only ones in the big park which could satisfy them.

Next day there was no sign of Pippa. She kept away for nine days, the longest time she had so far concealed her newly born litters from me. We searched all over the plain where we had last seen her, but neither spoor nor recent droppings gave us a clue as to her whereabouts. Then, on the 23rd, I suddenly saw her standing on the high ground behind the camp where I had parked my Land-Rover. She screened the surroundings for a very long time and I was glad to see her so suspicious. Pippa, who in her early youth had been a frequent guest in the Nairobi restaurants, now behaved far more like a wild animal than did the cheetah in the Amboseli and Nairobi National Parks which, having become so used to admiring tourists, frequently hop on to their cars and even tolerate being touched by them. I could not have asked for a greater reward for the loneliness I had experienced, which was the consequence of having kept visitors away from her right from the beginning of her rehabilitation, than to watch her now making sure we were undisturbed. Only after she was sure that no danger was present did she come near us, demanding meat. Then, by the way she wolfed it down, I could judge how hungry she was; I also saw how thin she had become. After finishing her meal, she instantly retraced her spoor along the road to Leopard Rock, by-passing the plain I had expected her to choose as a nursery.

It was midday and very hot, but Pippa walked quickly for two miles before she turned off and made her way some 500 yards through the bush in the direction of the Mulika rivulet. After sniffing carefully around, she led Local and me to a mellifera bush (the same 'wait-a-bit' acacia she had always used for her nurseries); hidden inside the thicket, I saw four cubs. Two had their eyes open and were bigger than the others. Remembering that in the case of her previous three litters the cubs had opened their eyes between the tenth and eleventh days, I assumed that these cubs were nine days old, therefore born on the 15th of July.

While watching the fluffy little creatures crawling on their very shaky legs to Pippa's teats, I could not help smiling at the way in which she had again fooled us so successfully by making us believe that she would choose the plain, half a mile from camp, for giving birth. In fact, on the 13th, as soon as we had left her with the elephants, she must have walked up here, where the grass was low and conditions ideal for rearing tiny cubs. There were plenty of thornbushes scattered around with enough open space between for her to watch out for danger. Both the Vasorongi and Mulika rivulets were within fifteen minutes' walk and her nursery was well hidden from the road, although she could hear a passing car or the lions, which often used the road as a highway, but always gave plenty of warning of their approach by their whuffings.

As I watched the family the little ones suckled for all they were worth, pressing their faces deep into Pippa's soft belly as she moved herself continuously into various positions to offer them the best supply of milk.

Reluctantly I left this peaceful scene and returned home.

Pippa knew by now that she could trust her newly born to Local and me, and when later that afternoon we again visited her she never stirred but kept on nursing the cubs for the brief time we stayed.

Judging by size only, there were two males amongst the four, but when I saw the three leathery, lentil-sized patches in triangular position, where later on the genitals of the males would grow, I concluded that in fact there were three males. If this were so, Pippa had kept a good balance between her second litter of three females and one male, and this present one with the opposite proportion of sexes. I had been unable to observe the relationships of male and female in her previous family because little Dume had died when barely five months old; so now I hoped that Pippa with my help would be able to rear the fourth family more successfully. Knowing from sad experience how prone young cheetah cubs are to leg injury, owing to their fragile bones, I was determined to prevent such accidents by adding vitamins to the cubs' food as soon as they started eating meat. Out of ignorance I had given such supplements too late to the previous litter. Already I had tried to help Pippa by adding a daily 15 mg of calcium lactate to her food during her pregnancy, and intended to continue to do so until she weaned her cubs.

Next morning I announced our arrival by calling Pippa from a distance. She emerged from her bush and walked over a hundred yards to a 'shady tree' where we fed her. She was extremely thirsty and could not drink enough, but she hardly touched her meat. I then noticed that her vulva was still blood-clotted, and I assumed her lack of appetite was due to the fact that she had not yet recovered from giving birth. Since she had reacted in the same way after she had borne her previous litters, this seemed to be normal and no cause for anxiety. Soon she sniffed the air and led me up-wind in a detour of some 300 yards to her cubs. They lifted their sleepy faces and lost no time in finding a teat as soon as their mother had licked each in turn and settled down. We left soon and only returned for a brief visit in the afternoon to bring more water to a very thirsty Pippa. Obviously she had not risked leaving her young alone to go to the river for a drink.

By the next day all the cubs had opened their eyes and, blinking vaguely at me, wrinkled their noses and spat. This reaction of wild cheetah cubs, when they sensed the presence of a creature which did not belong to their kind and realized that it might be dangerous, was familiar to me and what was interesting about it was that as yet they could hardly have had experience of danger. I also found it interesting to observe that Pippa now mistrusted good old Stanley, and would not come near her food while he was still in sight. Whereas usually, instead of wasting time to meet me first, she made a beeline for him when he was carrying the meat basket. I felt sorry for the poor fellow being so badly treated, but I remembered Elsa reacting in the same way after she had given birth; for quite a few weeks neither of her two African friends were allowed to appear even on the horizon.

Stanley accepted this temporary estrangement from Pippa good-naturedly, and despite her growls carried the heavy load of meat and water to her. Pippa daily increased the distances of her detour back to the nursery after eating, always taking great care that the direction of the wind should give the cubs her scent. On the thirteenth day after their birth she moved them within the bush to a different place, and did so again on the following day. But it took two more days before she carried them ten yards away to a new bush. I wondered why she was so cautious this time as she had moved her second and third litters to different localities within eleven days, while their eyes were still closed.

At their new home the cubs were far more in the open and, not being handicapped by dense thorns, toddled around vigorously. Pippa watched every one of their moves and when one of the quartet ventured off some nine feet on its own, she quickly pushed it back and spanked it gently.

One morning, while she sat under a nearby tree watching the surroundings, I tried to identify the sexes of the cubs by touching the genital parts, but all were still far too fluffy to ascertain the difference, although I still believed that there were three males, one of whom was much smaller than the female. I also took the opportunity to test their claws to see if at this early age they were retractable, for I knew that the Krefeld Zoo in Germany claimed them to be so for the first ten weeks. I had had only limited opportunities to prove their claim with Pippa's previous litter, but now I was determined to find out, and was finally able to make sure that cheetah claws were not retractable.

When the cubs were seventeen days old I heard them for the first time calling with a high-pitched chirp, to which Pippa instantly responded.

On the 1st of August Pippa came as usual to the 'Shady Tree' for her meal, and while she ate I went to see the cubs. They were fast asleep. I then followed Pippa to the road and on to the Vasorongi rivulet; here she searched for a suitable place where the water was shallow and she could drink without the risk of being nipped at by a crocodile; then, leaping in long bounds back to the road, she rolled for some time in the dust and finally walked off in a leisurely fashion, making a lengthy detour back to her cubs. Why I wondered was she so relaxed, did she know that they were still sleeping? They continued to sleep for another hour while Pippa and I rested close by.

Recently Pippa had waited for us on the road, using it in the early morning as a dust-bath. This worried me, not so much because of possible traffic, but because Pippa would leave her scent behind for predators to follow up. I was especially anxious one morning when I found the fresh spoor of three lions within my camp, which continued along the road for a mile towards Pippa's nursery. But when she met us at the 'Shady Tree' she seemed unconcerned and, after having eaten, led me to a bush much farther off in the plain and more secure as a nursery, than the previous one. I watched the cubs clambering amongst the bushes, probing each other and often tumbling over the thorny branches, until Pippa started nursing them and we left.

We had not gone more than 500 yards when we saw three lions walking along the road towards us. While we stopped to watch them, they bolted into the plain where, a little higher up, Pippa had her cubs. Very worried we did all we could to make them change their course. We must have been successful as the next morning we found the family under the same bush where we had left them, and found Pippa only concerned about the baboons which we heard barking not far away. She refused to eat her meal under the 'Shady Tree' and, looking nervously around, hardly touched the meat even after I had brought it close to the nursery . . . strangely, next morning she seemed not to be at all worried by the baboons which were still close, and even left the sleeping cubs for a long time in order to stretch her legs.

During her absence I investigated their teeth, and found the bottom incisors and the canines well developed. The cubs were three weeks old that day. Two days later the top incisors and canines had come through. Meanwhile Pippa had moved them some 250 yards into a very small bush which hardly offered any protection. Though the little ones could by now scramble along on their own it was a long distance for them to cover. I could not understand why Pippa had chosen this small bush and could understand it even less when I found the family still there on the following day, and Pippa very alert because of the two lions whose spoor we had seen along the road.

One of the cubs seemed puzzled by my presence, stared at me intensely and took up a defensive attitude, placing itself between me and his family. He kept on scrutinizing me until we left.

On my return to camp I found a message from George saying that he had met one of Pippa's daughters of a previous litter and said that if I came at once he might still be able to locate her. I drove over immediately and then went on with George to the place where he had seen the cub the day before. We stopped on the plain close to the Rojoweru River some three miles from his camp. Evidently the cub must have widened its territory, for when we had previously seen Whity and Tatu they had been nearer the camp. George told me that he had been searching for his lions when, standing on his car, calling and screening the surroundings with his binoculars, a cheetah had suddenly appeared and had sat down within twenty yards of him.

He offered her some meat, which she refused, so she could not have been very hungry, then he gave her water and while she lapped it from a bowl he took a few photographs. She was in excellent condition and disappeared soon after. Unfortunately we never found the cub that afternoon, but later on I identified her from the photographs as Whity.

I was still deeply attached to Mbili, Whity and Tatu, and wondered what by now Pippa's feelings were towards them. When they were young she had always shown great affection, licking and nursing them, and often she joined in their games. Invariably she had used great tact and gentleness so as not to arouse jealousy among them. Intermingled in close bodily contact, purring and showing every sign of contentment the family had always been happy and relaxed. Now, since these present cubs filled Pippa's life, the earlier ones seemed no longer to exist for her.

Does nature, I wonder, help wild animals to go on breeding litter after litter by cutting the ties between mother and young completely once they are able to live on their own? If not, how was it that neither Pippa nor her previous daughters had ever shown a wish to meet again? Can it be man's prerogative, alone amongst all mammals, to continue his relationship with the succeeding generations?

I was very conscious of the need to find the right answers to the many questions that cheetah pose, and for some time I had tried to co-opt a scientist to share my experiences and to complement my amateurish observations. But I had been warned that it might be impossible to combine the scientific method of studying animals, which is purely objective, and cuts out all personal relationships between animal and man, with my method which is subjective and primarily based on mutual trust and affection. In the end, as I failed to find a scientific colleague I could only try to use some of the ways that scientists had recommended to me, one of which was repeatedly to spend twenty-four hours with the animals and record minutely every detail of their behaviour; but it proved impossible to follow Pippa's movements during the night without disturbing her routine, so I had to be satisfied with spending all the hours of daylight with her and her family.

Luckily Pippa had by then moved the cubs into a bush large enough for me to sit close and watch everything the family did.*

By midday the heat became exceedingly trying, and although the lacy foliage of the *acacia mellifera* seemed to provide enough shade to keep the cheetah comfortable, I had to change my position under the thorny branches very often so as to keep in the shade and try and stop my headache. For the

* My notes can be found in Appendix I.

last hour I had been lying on my stomach with my head next to Pippa's, caressing her while she nursed her cubs and purred, then at 3.40 p.m. our idyll was suddenly interrupted by an aircraft circling low above us, obviously trying to locate us. Instantly the cheetah scattered, and I had great difficulty in leading the terrified cubs back into the bush and re-uniting them with Pippa.

A little later we heard the hooting of a car horn coming from the direction of the road. I sent Local to find out what all this meant; he returned with a note from a party from the London BBC who wanted to interview me at once as they had to fly back to Nairobi soon. Their visit had been arranged some time ago by the National Park Authorities, but it took me by surprise and put a full stop to my cheetah observations for that day. Hot and thirsty, I answered their questions, but refused to be photographed in my scruffy clothes which were very dirty from rolling all morning under thorny bushes – of course, what they were really interested in was photographing the cheetah, this I dodged tactfully. Against my principles I found myself committed to this interview, but it made me more determined than ever to keep strangers away from the family and avoid any publicity until my study of them was completed.

Next morning Pippa met us at the 'Feeding Tree' which was some distance from the bush where yesterday the plane had interfered with her routine. She ate in a leisurely way until faint chirping sounds made her look up. So far as I was concerned, these chirps could have been made by birds, but Pippa at once interrupted her meal and hurried off to her cubs. She had quite a job to find the little ones who, trying to follow her, had got entangled in the undergrowth and separated from each other. The smallest cub had an especially tough time struggling through the grass. When I found it panting and exhausted and crying for help, I picked it up. Feeling its silky fur for the first time, it was only with difficulty that I restrained myself from caressing it while carrying it some fifty yards to a bush under which Pippa was waiting with the rest of her family. This was a real thorny fortress with excellent shade. To me it seemed to be the perfect lair but Pippa was of a different opinion, and after walking restlessly around, ordered the cubs, in her mysterious way, to stay behind while she went off to find a better place. When she reappeared, she commanded them with a sharp prr prr to come along.

It was a charming sight to see the cubs trotting off in single file, winding their way through the grassy labyrinth until the smallest one was once again in trouble, as it tumbled against insurmountable obstacles. This time Pippa came to its rescue and carried it by the scruff of its neck, dropping it repeatedly to get a better grip as she picked it up again – until she reached a patch of open scrub in which she rested her young. I thought it a 'lousy' retreat, providing barely enough shade against the fierce sun, let alone security from predators. Pippa must have come to the same conclusion for leaving the little ones in my care she went off in search of a more suitable bush. She was away for twenty minutes, a long time for the cubs to wait, during which the smallest one came cuddling up to me, tempting me irresistibly to play with it. I needed to exert self-control not to respond to it and I was only just succeeding in not weakening when it joined the other cubs and all dozed off in a fluffy heap of soft bodies.

By now it was 10.00 a.m., the hour at which Pippa always suckled her cubs. She did not need a watch to tell her the time, and turned up at the exact minute. Strangely, however, she did not settle down to nurse the family, but went to the far end of the scrubby patch and lay down. I patted her and although she purred and seemed to like being caressed, she did not move. Expecting her to be thirsty after her long walk, I went back to the 'Feeding Tree' to collect water. On my return I found all the cheetah had disappeared. I searched under every promising bush for a long time, then I saw Pippa about 300 yards away coming towards me, alone and very thirsty. She drank the last drop of water, after which she returned to the 'lousy bush', where she stayed put. Nothing I could do would make her move back to her cubs, so, taking the hint, I went home. I wondered whether her restlessness, and her wish to hide the cubs was her reaction to my touching the smallest one, or if she were still upset about the plane circling so low and noisily yesterday above her lair? Whatever her reasons, I had to restore her trust which in either case had been injured by human interference.

2. The Danger of Milking a Puff-Adder

As soon as we reached camp, another plane circled low, then it headed towards the Kenmare airstrip two miles away, obviously wanting me to pick up its passengers there. Though I was surprised I could guess who the visitors were. Some time ago I had been approached by Sawyer-Viewmaster Stereo Pictures, USA, for my co-operation in making a new series about African animals in the name of Elsa. The well-known wildlife photographer, Alan Root, would take most of the pictures while I would add the ones of Pippa and her cubs. Since neither Alan Root nor I had ever handled a stereo camera Sawyer were sending their chief photographer, Fred Bennion, to Kenya to instruct us on the mechanism. I knew that Fred Bennion had recently arrived in the country.

When I drove up to the airstrip I found not only Bennion but also Alan Root and his wife Joan, together with their pilot, Ian Tippet, who often flew their private plane. I was glad to see Alan and Joan again, whom we had known then for many years, and we had followed their careers from the very beginning with great interest. Both being genuinely interested in wildlife, they had made superb films and still photographs for various people as well as working as freelances, and in the last few years they had travelled all over the world. We had not seen each other for some time, and I was greatly looking forward to hearing their latest news, so I was very disappointed when I learned that they intended to fly back to Nairobi that day.

While we prepared lunch at my camp I persuaded the party to spend the night. Fred Bennion had travelled several thousand miles from Oregon, USA to show me how to work a stereo camera, so I thought he might allow more than three hours for his visit to me and at the same time he could see something of the Meru Park. Neither he nor the Roots had been here before, and so we planned to visit George and his lions later in the afternoon.

While Fred Bennion demonstrated the camera to me the Roots went for a stroll. On their return I was terrified to see Alan with a large puff-adder coiled round his right arm which he was holding behind its head so that it could not strike. I have never pretended to be fond of snakes – especially not of puff-adders, which are one of the deadliest snakes in Africa, not only because of their quick-acting hematoxic venom, but also because of their ability to strike like a flash despite their normally slow, sluggish movements, which often prevent them from avoiding danger. Seeing how alarmed I was Alan assured me that he had handled snakes since he was a boy, and he also explained how he caught them by pinning their necks to the ground with a forked stick before picking them up behind their heads.

Local, Stanley and the cook had come close, their eyes and mouths were wide open, as they stared horror-struck at Alan and the puff-adder. Jokingly I told them that *Bwana* Root was a *muganga* (witch-doctor) who specialized in handling snakes; this made their eyes almost pop out of their sockets. Alan now wanted to show us the milking of the venom which I had never seen done. Quickly I got my cine camera and filmed the extraordinary performance from beginning to end. When Alan first placed a small stick between the upper and lower jaws to keep them apart I was amazed to see how they could open almost at a right angle. He then pushed the protective tissue back from one of the upper fangs, which it covered when not in action. As soon as the tooth was exposed the poison dribbled out in milky drops, enough to fill a dessert-spoon. Then Alan repeated the milking with the second fang until this too seemed empty.

By then the weight of the large puff-adder had tired Alan's arm and, believing that there was no venom left in either fang, he let the snake go. Instantly it wriggled to the nearest shelter which was the dining-hut. Hoping to prevent it entering the door, Alan rushed after it and tried to grab it quickly behind its head without a forked stick. He missed. He tried a second time and failed again to catch it. When he touched it for the third time the puff-adder struck and bit him in the right index finger. I would never have believed that any snake, let alone the puff-adder, could turn its head with such lightning speed in the opposite direction to that of its movements. While we were all concentrating on poor Alan the snake disappeared inside the hut and went underneath the shelf on which I kept the anti-snake bite outfits. As trade between Kenya and South Africa had come to a full stop some time ago, we had not been able to buy the Fitzsimon serum which we regarded as the best of all the anti-snake serums on the market. Instead I had one made by the Pasteur Institute and another of a German make, these I now offered to Alan for him to choose from, but he declined both saying that he was allergic to such remedies. He assured us that he could have received only a little poison since both the fangs had been completely drained, and that if he kept quiet for a while the venom would soon be absorbed. Nevertheless he asked to have a tourniquet put on, which we relaxed every twenty minutes. Since Alan was the snake expert amongst us we respected his wishes and, while he rested on a bed, listened to his stories. Meanwhile his wife read the instructions on the German preparation very carefully, and I gave him tea and glucose at frequent intervals, for he was very thirsty.

Despite his assurances that he would soon be fit enough to visit George, I did not like the look of his hand, which was swelling alarmingly, and suggested that he should fly back immediately to Nairobi to be in reach of a doctor, but he would have none of this and insisted that he would spend the night at the camp (and I assumed that he did this so that the rest of the party should not miss the visit to George). Since I could not force him against his will to fly in his own plane to

Nairobi, I was more than relieved when at this very moment a Land-Rover arrived, bringing Niels Larsen, one of our pilot friends who had previously flown visitors out to George and myself. Knowing how difficult it was for us to keep fresh fruit and vegetables, he most kindly presented me with a basket of grapes and other delicacies. He was due to return immediately with his client to Nairobi. His arrival seemed to me an act of Providence. I quickly took him aside and explained the situation, whereupon he offered to take Alan and Joan back at once. Paying no attention to Alan's protests, we succeeded in making him and Joan take off with Larsen and gave them the German serum in case an emergency arose.

After they had left I sighed with relief, for I was sure that Alan was much worse than he wanted to admit, and that he was adopting a carefree attitude partly to keep up his spirits and partly so as not to spoil our evening with George.

Knowing that we had done the best we could for Alan, we decided to go over to see George, but before doing so Ian Tippet most gallantly caught the puff-adder. He insisted on letting it live, so we secured it in a cardboard box and released it on our way. During the drive we watched three Lesser Kudu, one of the most attractive but shyest of the antelopes, stepping gracefully out of thick bush and posing for a photograph right in front of us. We also saw reticulated giraffe and buffalo, and many smaller animals. The track led through doum palm patches and the wide open plain, all looked very peaceful in the light of the setting sun.

By the time we reached George we knew that Alan must be landing in Nairobi and we hoped that he would be safe. Unfortunately we did not see the lions George was looking after, but even without the presence of the king of beasts, Fred Bennion was quite overwhelmed by all the animals he saw for the first time in their natural environment, and at once began to plan a holiday trip to Africa.

Next morning Ian Tippet had to fly to Nairobi to attend a meeting, but he was to return in the afternoon with the Roots so that they could spend a day of rest with us after Alan's nasty experience. Meanwhile, Fred Bennion remained with me. When Ian Tippet appeared alone, at teatime, we knew that something had gone wrong. He told us that as soon as the plane had taken off, Alan had become so violently ill that Joan had had to inject the full dose of the anti-venom serum into him and by the time they landed in Nairobi, he was delirious. The three doctors waiting for him at the hospital doubted if he would reach the hospital alive; his arm was extremely swollen and almost black, his pulse was hardly beating, and he was only kept alive with drugs. As soon as he was strong enough to stand the operation, they feared that his arm would have to be amputated. Meanwhile, all we could do was to pray for his life.

By one of the strangest coincidences, Ionides, the world authority on snakes, was lying in the next room to Alan. He had undergone an operation from which he was never to recover. Upon hearing the details of the accident, he was horrified by the combination of mistakes which led to Alan's collapse. To start with, Ionides could not conceive how anyone could think of catching any snake without a forked stick, let alone a puff-adder which was able to strike back at an angle of 180°. Secondly, it was a fallacy to believe that a puff-adder's fangs were empty after milking, for the ducts were instantly refilled with a far more potent poison than the one that had been milked off, which might have been some time in the fangs and thus become weaker. Thirdly, one should never use a tourniquet for hematoxic snakes, because of the poison – being concentrated into a small part of the body it destroys the tissues and flesh much more quickly. So poor Alan had been a victim of our ignorance: apart from this two vital hours had been lost before his wife had been able to inject the anti-poison serum during the flight. The next four months were ones of great anxiety for Joan and Alan, but his arm was saved, and also his hand, by specialists on snake-bite cases who were flown in from South Africa. Finally he was treated in

England. Because the tissues had been destroyed by the poison he did lose his right index finger but he trained himself to continue his photographic career with four fingers only.

However scared I have been of snakes after this ghastly accident, I shall always maintain that snakes are not aggressive until provoked, which was undoubtedly the case when Alan milked this puff-adder. It was also interesting to remember that in the first year that I camped here, I killed snakes almost daily during the rainy seasons, but that since then, the H I S S must have got round amongst the snakes that my camp is no safe refuge despite the tempting hiding-places it provides, for they have almost ceased to invade us.

If we humans take precautions against snakes, animals also try to protect themselves and their young against them. I was fascinated when George's cook told us the story of a scene he had watched a short time ago. He was resting in his hut during the hot hours after lunch when he heard a strange noise, like something slithering against the wire enclosure which surrounds his quarters. He went out to investigate and saw a red cobra with a tiny rat in its mouth, being fiercely attacked by the mother rat. As he watched, the rat grabbed the cobra behind its head and inflicted a severe bite. The cobra thrashed about, endeavouring to rid itself of its assailant, who, despite being violently thrown around, retained its grip and hung on, until the cobra managed to reach a hole. Only when the rat was brushed against the edge of it, did it let go and the snake disappeared. Unfortunately the baby rat was dead by then, despite the courageous defence by its mother.

3.   A Death in the Family

It was now the peak of the tourist season, which I enjoyed, provided that the visitors did not interfere with the cheetah. This was essential if Pippa's cubs were to grow up as wild animals. Of course I was not always popular, because the tourists could not understand why I refused to take them to see the family. But I have always kept to my principle that wild animals must never be conditioned to lose their fear of man.

Pippa seemed to share my attitude, and disapproved if even I took greater familiarities with her children than she considered fair.

One day they were most interested in me, brushing themselves deliberately against my legs and toddling close around me, ignoring Pippa's prr prr and evident wish that this game should stop. Three times she carried them into a thicket, but the cubs were equally determined and sauntered back as soon as she dropped them. The smallest cub was especially friendly and followed me wherever I went. When Pippa made no attempt to suckle her young at her usual time (10.00 a.m.) I left. Next morning I placed myself, well hidden from the cubs, behind a bush and watched them climbing on to Pippa's back and sliding off the other side, nibbling at her ears until a jerk of her head sent them flying. Then they rolled playfully to the ground, holding each other down, spanking and biting, or sitting on each other's heads till their mother came to the rescue, licking and purring, and they all settled for their meal sharp at 10.00 a.m. Seeing Pippa today so much at ease, perhaps because she knew I was close yet not interfering with her young, I was impressed but also puzzled that she seemed to want our friendship to be restricted to herself. Was this due to an instinct to preserve the natural relationship between herself and her family, despite the fact that she had trusted me and had accepted me as her foster-mother since she had been six months old? She demonstrated a similar attitude on the following day when I found the family under a new bush. The plain was more open here, the grass shorter and the cubs could move about more easily.

On my arrival Pippa emerged and sniffed at the meat, then she returned quickly to the cubs. After reassuring herself that they were well hidden, she led me nearly 100 yards away before eating. She had never objected to Local being near whilst she had her meal, so I was surprised to see her growling and returning hurriedly to her family when he approached us.

By next morning she had moved to a large acacia with low hanging branches forming a shady dome over a termite hill, and surrounded by such thick undergrowth that it was impossible to see the cheetah unless they moved. At last I detected the cubs, who kept absolutely still. Some time later Pippa turned up from the direction of the Mulika River, looked suspiciously around, and, after making sure the cubs were safe, walked off again. I followed her for fifteen minutes, repeatedly offering her meat, but she ate so little that when she returned to the cubs I placed the remains on the ground. That, evidently, was the last thing she wanted me to do, and looking in the opposite direction she soon retired deep inside the lair. Meanwhile the cubs came to investigate the new scent and cautiously approached the meat, but when quite close they wrinkled their noses in disgust and spat at it. Soon after this, I left.

At teatime I again tried my luck, and was surprised to find Pippa waiting for us at some distance from her lair, for this was an unusual hour for us to visit her. She was extremely thirsty and quickly lapped the water we had brought before returning, in wide circles, to the cubs. When we came within fifty yards of them she looked hard at Local, stopped dead and would not budge until I sent him back. Only after he was out of sight did she go to her cubs and suckle them.

The following morning we searched for two hours before we almost stepped on the family right in the open. I offered Pippa meat some distance away from her children, but she barely nibbled at it and seemed more interested in finding cover for them. It looked as if we had caught them on their way to the Mulika River because she soon moved on again in that direction, the little ones toddling behind as best they could except for the smallest one which Pippa had to carry for most of the distance. Although she gazed longingly towards the Mulika she had to give the cubs a rest, and then at last consented to eat. Remembering that only yesterday the cubs were pulling faces at the meat, it was astonishing now to see one of the males tearing so heartily at it that Pippa nipped him frequently to prevent him from eating too much. The cubs were five weeks old that day, and this was exactly the age at which Whity, Mbili and Tatu had first touched meat. It took three more days for the other cubs to join in the new diet, during which time Pippa moved to several new lairs.

Since the cubs now ate meat I took great care to leave no trace of it behind which might attract predators, and always placed it on a piece of canvas so that no scent should infiltrate the ground. Pippa had always been a perfect mother, and therefore I could not understand why she now cuffed the cubs as soon as I put the meat in front of them, or calling prr prr, moved off before they could eat. They were keen enough and their teeth sufficiently well developed to tackle meat, but often they had to be content with chewing at sticks instead. Why, I wondered, did she prevent them from eating meat? The little ones were thin but very lively and played vigorously in the early mornings, only settling down to sleep when the sun became too hot.

It was not until six days after the cubs had shown their first interest in meat that Pippa made a point of showing them how to eat it. She sucked the intestines into her mouth between her teeth, thus squeezing out the contents. She also demonstrated how to lap water from the bowl, but the cubs were not too good at that for a few days.

The family had lately moved on to a more open part of the plain with isolated bushes scattered round. They were ideal lay-ups since, hidden inside their dense foliage and well protected from the sun, Pippa could detect the slightest danger approaching from long distances. I was therefore amazed when we found the place one morning occupied by a herd of seven elephants, two of them right next to the bush from which Pippa emerged to get her meal. She ate it, apparently unconcerned about the elephants who browsed for some ten minutes off the bush under which her cubs were hidden. Even when one of these giants churned up the earth with his front leg into a cloud of dust she showed no anxiety but quietly chewed away. We had to wait what seemed a very long time for the elephants to move far enough for us to get near the cubs. Judging by the spoor these giants had been within two yards of the family for a long time. By the time we reached them the little ones were very hungry and fought for their share. They even defended their meat from Pippa so that they could drag it deep inside the bush where they felt safe to eat it. Once they had had their fill they jumped playfully on their mother as if she were a rock, tearing at her skin and ears in no gentle way: but she seemed to love this game and, closing her eyes, purred the more the cubs maltreated her head.

During the next day the elephant became a nuisance as far as we were concerned. Often we had to wait a long time before we could look under promising bushes where the family might be concealed, only to find that Pippa had kept, apparently quite deliberately, right amongst the herd. She had never shown fear of pachyderms – rhino, hippo, elephant – and obviously she was making good use of them now to protect her family from a troop of baboons which had also invaded the place.

One morning we looked for many hours for the cheetah,

especially in the vicinity of three thornbushes which had recently been their lair. We saw no sign of the family, but found six elephants persistently besieging the bushes. Exhausted, we gave up at midday. When at teatime we continued our search we found one elephant still guarding the three bushes, from which Pippa soon emerged in response to my calls. Simultaneously six elephants came thundering and trumpeting across the plain, but luckily swerved off in the opposite direction as soon as they got our scent, while the single one moved towards the road. I offered Pippa only the small piece of meat which concealed her daily dose of calcium, and withheld the rest of her meal hoping that she would show us her cubs. But she was no fool and stubbornly refused to move until it was almost dark, and I had to give in. After she had eaten she walked extremely carefully, avoiding making any sound, even the breaking of a twig, for about three-quarters of a mile towards the road, where we caught up with the single elephant. Anxiously I looked for the cubs, and found them well concealed in the high grass almost at my feet. Quickly I placed the meat in front of them but they remained immobile until Pippa called prr prr, after which they rushed for it. It was now quite dark, and being concerned about the safety of the cubs eating in such an open place, we sat with them until they had finished their meal. This took some time for, with their small teeth, they could chew only very slowly and I had to divert Pippa's interest so that she should not take advantage of this delay to finish off the meat. While listening to their munchings I heard for the first time a cub imitating Pippa's prr prr.

They were now six weeks old and had been moved to fourteen different lairs up to date, but never once so long a distance as today. Since they could all walk quite well I assumed they had outgrown their early nursery stage. They were a lovely quartet: the two big males, one slightly larger than the other and very plucky, always kept close together and already had an air of self-assurance which the two smaller cubs lacked especially the female who was very nervous and often sat apart while the brothers played together. But all were most affectionate and always cuddled up to Pippa, who was devoted to them.

Early next morning I found the cheetah at the same place, still close to the single elephant; Pippa was keeping a look-out from a fallen tree. The big male cub clambered up to her, but although he tried hard to keep his balance he fell off several times. Then he lapped the water from the bowl with great gusto. After all had eaten, the family gambolled to the road, and settled for their midday rest within a hundred yards of it under a bushy tree. I was worried at leaving the cubs so close to the road and returned in the afternoon hoping to entice them for a walk and get them moving into the plains. But Pippa seemed tense, and kept hiding deep inside the bush and would not budge.

All night I felt extremely anxious and as soon as it was light we went to look for them but found the place deserted. Instead we saw fresh lion spoor not far along the road. We screened the area for about half-an-hour until Pippa appeared, coming from 'Mile 5' where the Mulika crosses the road. Sniffing the ground, she led me in a roundabout way to a bushy tree, but then sat put at some distance while I walked around it. When I reached the other side, hidden from Pippa, my heart stood still for there I saw the big male cub, dead – bitten through his neck. He lay close to the bush and there was no trace of blood on the grass, or any sign of a fight. The blood on his wound was still fresh when I picked up the slightly stiffened body to take it to the car. Pippa did not see what I was carrying and walked on.

Local and I followed her as she went sniffing along the road in the opposite direction from which she had come. After some 200 yards we saw her morning tracks mixed up with the spoor of the cubs. Here she turned off in the direction of the three bushes. Sniffing the ground even more intensely, and climbing every tree and termite hill, she scrutinized the surroundings with hard eyes, then she settled near a bush from which she did not move although she listened constantly and watched for any slight movement. I took the opportunity to send Local for her food. After Local had brought her the meat, she took so long to eat it that I feared her other cubs were also dead. Finally she moved off, and as we passed a twinbush I heard a wee sound coming from it, like the chirping of a bird. Ignoring this Pippa walked on while I had a good look inside the foliage where I detected the three cubs. Pippa stopped some hundred yards farther on and rested there for a good half-hour, always listening alertly for more chirps. We could not understand her behaviour. Did she not trust us and was she unwilling to give away the whereabouts of her surviving cubs? This seemed to be confirmed when, later on, she returned to the road and carefully avoided the twinbush. As soon as we reached the turn-off where her cub had been killed, she sat down.

Leaving Local behind to watch her movements I now went along the road up to 'Mile 5' looking for more traces of the disaster. Here I found Pippa's spoor, for some 300 yards inter-mingled with the pugmarks of a lioness or young lion until both had turned in opposite directions – Pippa towards the Mulika plain where I now knew she kept her cubs concealed. Trying to discover from the spoor how the tragedy had hap-pened, I assumed that when the lion came along the road he scented the cheetah and went to the bushy tree. The big and plucky male cub may have crawled out to protect his family, as he had tried to do before when I had come too close, and been instantly killed. Meanwhile Pippa must have left the bush at the far side and got chased by the lion until their spoor left the road in opposite directions. She may then have re-turned to her cubs, and may even have carried them to the spot where we found their spoor together on the road. After hiding them in the twinbush half a mile off it, she probably then went back up to 'Mile 5' to look for the missing cub. It was from here she had come when we arrived. She still seemed not to know that he would never return to her.

When I rejoined Local and Pippa on the road, she walked back to her cubs. I asked Local to remain behind and she led me in a straight line to the twinbush which was now guarded by the single elephant. To give him time to move away, I collected meat and water for the cubs, and on my return found the elephant gone. Soon after this Pippa called prr prr, and in response the cubs came crawling out of the bush, but they were extremely nervous. Even when Pippa encouraged them by demonstrating how to eat the intestines in spaghetti fashion, they nibbled very carefully, looking around constantly. The female was especially frightened and bolted back to the bush if I made the slightest movement. So as not to upset the family further by my presence I left and drove to the Park Warden to tell him what had happened. We both examined the teeth of the dead cub and found that at six weeks and four days all his molars were already through. Then I took the cub to my camp to bury it there. While the men were digging the grave I held the little cheetah. How beautiful it was, so clean despite the horrible wound behind his head! I decided to sketch him before burying him, and so keep part of him with me.

While I was painting the strongest and most beautiful of Pippa's four cubs I tried to understand why such a perfect animal at the beginning of his life should be deprived of it for no apparent reason. There seemed to be no logical answer other than the fact that any full-grown predator often kills the young of other predatory species to eliminate a rival. Several times we had found lion cubs killed by leopards, and vice versa; the victim was always left untouched. In this case the cub's pluck might have been the cause of his death. Strangely, while I was absorbed in my sketching my anguish relaxed, and the more the portrait of the dead body seemed to live on the paper, the less pain I felt. I cannot explain the strange transition I went through, but by the time the sketch was finished, the pang of death had gone.

We buried the little cub under the tree where Pippa had

often rested with her family.

On our way to find the cheetah next morning Local was walking a few steps behind me on the road when suddenly a lion jumped out of the grass and charged him. While he tore the rifle from his shoulder and clattered the bolt into position, the lion came within five yards of him, and now I recognized Ugas, George's one-eyed lion! Instantly I called 'No, no, Ugas, stop!' and in the nick of time prevented what might well have been a tragedy. Local would have been justified in shooting Ugas in self-defence, but luckily it was not necessary for Ugas obeyed me and sank back into the high grass again. He must have rested near to the road, and may have been taken by surprise when we passed close by him. Nevertheless we were rather shaken, especially as all this had happened within 200 yards of where Pippa's cubs had been killed.

I did not like having Ugas so close to Pippa, so I drove the twelve miles to George's camp and asked him to try and entice Ugas back to his domain. Ugas had frequently been near my camp and even right inside it, which did no harm as long as I was there and could call George to control him, but with Pippa's cubs around the situation had changed. We arranged that George should bring some meat and with it try to induce Ugas to jump inside the wired-in pick-up Land-Rover and be driven home. But although George spent the night at my camp waiting ready with the baited car, Ugas was far too preoccupied with a wild lioness to show up. It was probably the same lioness that had killed Pippa's cub as George later found them mating within a mile of where the tragedy had taken place.

Meanwhile, for the next two days we searched in vain for Pippa. Although this did not surprise me, these days were most exhausting, physically and mentally. While screening every bush I found a young cerval cat hiding in one. Realizing that she had no escape from me, she kept absolutely frozen and only her terrified eyes proved that she was alive. Staring at me from no more than two feet away she remained completely immobile for about ten minutes. By this time she had made me believe that she was ill, and I left to find Local so that we might help her. On our return she was gone. Shamming death by freezing is a well-known reaction of any cornered animal, but I admired the self-control of this cerval cat in keeping completely still for so long a time and at such close range until she found it safe to run away.

But where was Pippa? We were searching amongst shoulder-high reeds along the Mulika when a lion growl made us stop abruptly. By the moving of the reeds we knew that we had almost stepped on the lion who was probably asleep. Soon after this we had another narrow escape by startling a buffalo from his midday rest. It was exhaustingly hot and he was lying underneath a bush which we were just going to investigate. Like the lion, he had enough room for retreat and so we were able to continue our search.

It was only in the evening of the third day that we located Pippa not far from the Mulika, yet she must have heard us calling day after day. She was extremely hungry and so must her cubs have been, but she did not allow them to appear while she had an enormous meal and finally we had to return without seeing them.

I could understand Pippa's fear of exposing her children after dark, and from now on I made every effort to feed the family when possible in the mornings. The cubs ate only a little at a time, but liked to feed at frequent intervals throughout the day. Therefore I repeatedly spent all the daylight hours with the family, cutting the meat into thin slices so that the cubs could gobble it all up before Pippa could interfere. I was puzzled that she should prevent the hungry cubs from having their fill as I always brought more food than she could eat. Looking up my notes I saw that she had completely weaned her previous litter at eight weeks, while her present cubs at the same age still lived mainly on milk. The female especially needed a lot of coaxing to take her fair share of meat, which often proved very difficult owing to her shyness.

Local once suggested that I should call in the Big Doctor to give her a *sindano* so that she would get strong like her two brothers. He, like most uneducated Africans, believed in the magical power of the sindano, which means needle in Swahili but in this case syringe. Whatever illness he himself might be suffering from, one perhaps which needed different treatment, no cure could, to his way of thinking, be as effective as a prick with the sindano, even if it was only filled with water. Local also believed that a superior intelligence could be developed from the use of powerful sindanos, and that it was merely a matter of having enough money to pay for it.

I counted rather on the use of the right supplements, and therefore increased the doses of Farex, Abidec and bonemeal to enable the little female to stand up to the bullying of her brothers who were often very boisterous with her.

Usually the family fed as soon as we arrived in the morning and their meal lasted for about one and a half hours. Then, despite their full stomachs, the cubs chased each other around and were often joined by Pippa who herself hopped and gambolled like a cub until all were tired. When the cubs dozed off Pippa kept a drowsy guard for an hour or so until they woke up to have their second meal. After which they again played off their heaviness for a short while before they all fell deep asleep during the midday heat. This was the safest time as only the most hungry predators would prowl around during the hot hours when the air was shimmering, and not the faintest sound betrayed any activity.

Now we thought it time to name the cubs; we decided to call the female Somba, the large male Big Boy, and his small brother Tiny. Tiny was my favourite. Not only because he was almost a replica in looks and character of Mbili, my favourite of Pippa's previous litter, but also because he too was the runt. He had charm and courage to make up for his physical inferiority, as well as the most beautiful, expressive eyes.

Big Boy was also most attractive but in a different way. Not only was he exceptionally handsome and the best-tempered of

he cubs, but his self-assurance radiated leadership, and even
at this age he was unquestionably the boss.

Somba was the most intelligent, but the most complicated
character of the trio. Being aware of her weakness she com-
pensated for it with a feminine defensive instinct. She had a
way of hunching up into an almost springing attitude, her eyes
looking out at an awkward angle from under her lowered head
until she was ready to strike with both her front legs simultaneously. How she could do this without tumbling over I
could not imagine, but it was a most effective defence and
small as she still was, I did not dare move when she was in
such a mood. She practised this tactic especially when I had
given her the complete head of a carcass. Did she associate
this with a natural kill, even though she had not yet – to my
knowledge – experienced one? I was also interested to see
that the cubs closed their eyes whenever they concentrated on
crushing small bones. I knew that I also shut my eyes while
concentrating, for instance when talking into a microphone or
when dictating, so I supposed that closing one's eyes is an aid
to concentration.

When Big Boy was eleven weeks and five days old, I saw
him for the last time suckling Pippa. Suspecting that he did
this merely for comfort, from now on I squeezed Pippa's teats
daily and found to my amazement that she went on lactating
until the cubs were twenty-four weeks and three days old. This
was the age at which Pippa's previous litter had shown slight
signs of rickets and at which they suffered from three broken
legs. I was very glad to see that no such symptoms were
apparent in her present cubs, who were superbly fit and full of
energy.

4. Fire and Flood

It was now the beginning of October and the long rains were not far off. Shortly before they broke, it was the usual practice in National Parks to burn off the old grass to make room for the new, and thus also kill the parasites which harm the game. In order to control the fires around my camp, I had asked the Warden to send a labour-gang to set the plains alight. When the men arrived with torches made of palm fronds, I had no need to order my staff to help – quite the contrary, they were so keen to kindle fires everywhere that I had to watch out they did not burn the camp. They thoroughly enjoyed throwing matches into the dry grass in spite of the fact that in the process they got nearly suffocated and their eyes smarted from the crackling flames. Watching them having their fun, I reflected that arson as a crime might spring from the same sense of enjoyment that primitive people derive from such a fire as this.

Of course grass fires were not new to Pippa, but the cubs seemed terrified by the faintest scent of smoke, especially Somba who was always on the alert sniffing the air. For the last few days the family had been near the Mulika where they had found an ideal playground on a termite hill overshadowed by a tree. Here the cubs soon discovered a new game: tobogganing down the hill and playing hide-and-seek between the air funnels. They also enjoyed endless games of 'Who is King of the Hole' as they competed for a large depression on the hill which provided a comfortable bed for just one cub. Standing on their hind legs to give the fullest impact to their weight, they bounced on the owner of the hole until he was pushed out of it. But best of all the fun was jumping back and forth across the rivulet and they soon found out how to do this without landing in the water.

When the fires began to close in, Pippa lost no time in taking the cubs to safety. Even though the flames were still far away, they were so scared that, in their eagerness to escape, they splashed into the rivulet, all their skilful jumping forgotten. Then they scrambled to safety on to the far bank and disappeared. It was interesting to see the family's reaction to the fires, compared with that of the predators we' had watched in the Serengeti. There, the lions especially had sat so close to the leaping flames, waiting for escaping animals or warming themselves, that they sometimes got singed by flying sparks.

During the burning many animals temporarily left their territories but how far they went I only realized when I saw a herd of six Lesser Kudu near my camp one morning. Normally these beautiful antelopes live in thick bush some ten miles away and these must have crossed the crocodile-infested Rojoweru River. I only saw them on this one occasion, and assumed that they left this open country again as soon as the fires had abated.

For the next two days we could not find the family. On our searches we looked at a dry water-hole and I tried to walk over the hard, cracked surface only to sink knee-deep into almost liquid mud which gave way like quick-sand at every move I made. Sinking rapidly deeper and deeper, I yelled for Local, who, luckily, was near enough to hand me a long pole with which he pulled me out. Without his help I would have had no chance of freeing myself from the sucking liquid, which had looked so solid on the surface.

Finally we found the cheetah hiding inside the three bushes. We only detected them because one of the cubs gave the family away by a faint chirp. We had been driving the car across the cinder-blackened plain and our stopping near the bushes may have frightened him. All looked most bewildered at the ashy desert around them, and Pippa was extremely nervous about showing them in the open where their golden colour was now very conspicuous against the blackened ground. Little

Somba was especially agile and, even though barely three months, watched out as sharply as Pippa for the slightest sign of a distant fire. If she saw one she ran off instantly. Lately she had become surprisingly fierce and obviously knew the effect her crouching-striking act had on everybody. Even Pippa kept her distance at these times.

I had given meat to the family, which they had eaten ravenously. Afterwards, while they were playing, Pippa tried to get hold of Somba's head, but the little cat rolled growling round and round, never letting her mother out of her sight, till suddenly she sprang up and struck out in a fury; Pippa only avoided the blow by jumping off the ground with all four legs at once. Somba struck again and again, while Pippa kept on hopping off the ground, until she moved away. Instead of putting her belligerent daughter in her place, she waited until Somba settled down. Then, after a little while, the cub embraced her mother in such a disarming way that both rolled together happily, all bad temper forgotten.

I had to be very tactful not to provoke Pippa's jealousy by feeding the cubs first. She resented this deeply and whether or not they had eaten, would move away, calling prr prr for the cubs to follow her. The more Somba developed her crouching-striking act, the less inclined was Tiny to fight for his share. Fighting for food is normally a good stimulus for making a cub eat even if it is not hungry, but Tiny realized that he could not stand up to Somba's tricks and simply walked to one side, waiting for me to hand-feed him. This soon became routine, and he watched carefully how and where I concealed his share from the rest of the family, and then waited for an opportunity to eat undisturbed. All loved the fat of zebra and the trachea of any carcass, in which I often concealed the bone-meal which the cubs disliked. To prevent me from spoiling their favourite food Somba often struck at me when she saw me sprinkling bonemeal on to these titbits.

Fires had been raging all over the region which Pippa frequented and the only area which was no longer smouldering was the plain across the Vasorongi, some four miles upstream from my camp, to which Pippa now took her cubs. There we found them one morning on a freshly killed young Grant's gazelle. Pippa had suffocated it by compressing its throat, otherwise the carcass was still untouched. As soon as I came near Somba charged most aggressively, lunging at me, spitting and growling, with such murderous eyes that I was truly scared. Of course I was glad that she reacted like a wild animal to her first 'natural' kill, or rather, like a female, whose business it is to defend the kill; the males did not mind my being there. To my surprise, when I held out the milk to the cubs Somba quickly joined her brothers, but if I dared to move towards her kill, she charged immediately. Unfortunately I had not brought the cine camera, so leaving Local in charge of the family, I collected it from camp. On my return the cheetah had not finished the kill and Somba was defending it as fiercely as in the morning.

Meanwhile the air was heavy with rain and dark clouds hung like curtains ready to burst at any moment. The frequent thunder claps terrified the cubs who bolted at the slightest rumbles, until finally Pippa called prr prr and they all moved off. We collected the remains of the Grant, to save it for the next day's meal, and returned home.

The cheetah stayed for a week on this part of the plain which we could only reach by wading through the flooded rivulet whose depth increased daily. After one night of very heavy rain we could no longer cross it. Luckily we soon found the spoor of the family on our side – they must have swum across just in time. I assumed that Pippa had done this so as not to be cut off from her meat supply, but she proved to me once again how little I could read her mind. Instead of moving near to my camp where she knew that I had meat, she took the cubs two miles in the opposite direction on to a plain where there were lots of Grant and zebra. This obviously proved that she preferred her cubs to grow up wild, and not get used to our camp.

They gave us another proof of how wild they were when we spotted them one morning within 300 yards of the Land-Rover. Leaving the vehicle on the road, we carried the meat to the hungry family. While they tucked in a tourist car appeared, but long before it reached our Land-Rover the cubs had bolted out of sight, in spite of not having finished their meal.

Now, for the first time since they had parted months ago, Pippa was in Mbili's territory. The only reason I could imagine for the breaking of her self-imposed rule was that most of the surrounding country had recently turned into swamps where it was extremely difficult to hunt. I found it interesting to observe that Pippa never used the same trees or anthills she had frequented when with Mbili, Whity and Tatu, but chose new playgrounds for her present cubs; these tree-stumps she marked carefully for several days with her droppings. Did she do this to establish her territory? I wondered what would happen if Mbili should turn up?

One morning, after we had fed the family, Pippa stared with tightly closed lips towards a distant ridge. Following the direction, I saw, through my field-glasses, two white rhino very far away. They belonged to the three pairs which had been imported from South Africa three years ago in the hope of rehabilitating them and breeding from them in Kenya. For the time being, these six rhino were kept inside a large enclosure at Leopard Rock from which these two had obviously escaped. The white rhino differ from the black by being of a larger size and having a wider mouth. Hence their name 'White', which originates from a Dutch misspelling of 'wide'. I did not know if these differences were enough to frighten Pippa, but, prr prr, and she and her cubs bolted as fast as they could run. I was interested to know if she could differentiate between the two species, and if she had run away from the one unfamiliar to her although she usually ignored the local, black rhino. I had to wait for more than a year to get the confirmation from her cubs who then reacted in exactly the same way.

The cheetah's spoor led us back to Pippa's territory on the Mulika plain where we found them intermingled with the fresh spoor of lion. Therefore I was not surprised that we could not find the family for a few days. Finally Stanley spotted a cheetah trotting, growling, towards him from the direction of 'Mile 5'. Surprised by this, he called me. On seeing me the cheetah leapt around in a strange manner, and then kept running through the bush with frequent stops to make sure we were following, but it never let me come close enough to identify it. While engaged in this wait-and-catch game the cheetah flushed two guinea-fowl and jumped into the air to catch them, but missed both times. I assumed the cheetah must be Pippa, having hidden her cubs from the lions and wanting to lead me to them, so I struggled on for fifteen minutes. By then I had become very worried as never before had Pippa left the cubs alone and gone such a long distance away from them. At last I nearly caught up with the cheetah, but was still too far off to identify it. There was no sign of the cubs. Fearing the worst, I called 'Pippa'. Instantly, the cheetah bolted towards the Mulika, jumped across and disappeared. Now it dawned on me that this must be Mbili, since Pippa would never behave like this. I was very happy to see Mbili so fit after having lived on her own for eight and a half months. She was in Pippa's territory, but this could be explained by the presence of a labour-gang working along her frontier and this might well have frightened her and caused her to cross it.

Later on we found the family within half a mile, all well. There were quite a lot of animals to hunt and Pippa tried her best to stalk a herd of Grant, but she could never get close enough as all the cover was now burnt. Again I wondered what would happen if she were to meet Mbili? Next morning I found the family close to the place where Mbili had disappeared; all were looking round frequently as though waiting for something.

They were six miles from the camp, close to the road, so the following morning we covered the distance by car and parked about 400 yards off the road, when we spotted a herd of Grant running towards us. Soon after this the family appeared. While we prepared the food for them Pippa vanished, but she seemed to have ordered the cubs to sit put so effectively that I had to carry the meat to them, though they had watched me cutting it up. While they tucked in Pippa reappeared and sat down near a bush some fifty yards away, calling the cubs in a low voice. She was panting heavily when I took meat to her, and I noticed blood on her right front paw and on her mouth. She was very irritable and would not allow me to examine her foot but kept on looking towards the road and did not touch the meat. Soon, she left and settled near the road. Meanwhile I had sent the men to search for a kill; when they returned without having found one, I took milk over to Pippa. Now I understood her behaviour – for I found her guarding the carcass of a young Grant which she had suffocated. She had obviously tried to make what had happened clear to me by leaving the kill and calling me to explain that she did not like leaving the carcass next to the road – but I had failed to understand her. I carried the kill far into the plain where she could eat it undisturbed by possible traffic.

As soon as the cubs spotted it, they danced around it, very excited, and Pippa let them play with it for a long time. But when they failed to open the carcass she demonstrated the best way to do it – by starting between the hind legs where the skin is soft and there are no bones.

I was fascinated by Somba's behaviour. As soon as I moved towards the kill she charged more fiercely than she had ever done before, spitting with lowered head and striking at me rapidly with both front legs simultaneously. I retreated carefully backwards, step by step, with Somba following me and striking repeatedly. But when she saw her brothers busy at the kill, she rushed over so as not to miss anything and chased them off. To compensate the boys we offered them the meat we had brought, only to see Somba coming quickly along to get her share, which she even took from my hand. When I moved again towards the kill she almost dropped the meat out of her mouth to strike at me and stop me from going a step farther. She repeated this performance all day until we left. Poor Somba, I sympathized with her confusion; here I was, one moment the trustworthy provider of food who fed her daily with well prepared meat, and then the next moment I violated her wild instincts which urged her to defend a natural kill. So, torn between two impulses which she could not reconcile, she changed instantly from a friendly creature eating out of my hand into a very dangerous, wild cheetah. All this was aggravated by being not only a female, whose defensive instincts are more developed than those of the males, but also by knowing that she was physically weaker than they which made her very alert to being left out of anything the brothers might have got hold of. It was because of this that she appeared unjustifiably greedy. So as not to encourage her aggressiveness, I made a point from now on of always feeding her first and letting her have the pieces she preferred.

I learned a lot from Pippa about how to handle all her cubs. She respected their different characters, but disciplined them though with great tact. Lately Somba had seemed to be at war not only with me but with the whole family. She behaved so dangerously I sometimes even contemplated having to destroy her; but watching how Pippa coped with her belligerent daughter, always managing in the end to put her at ease, I realized that I had no right to interfere.

The more I knew of Pippa the more I loved her. She had only fully developed her endearing character after she had borne cubs. How she succeeded in adjusting herself to their constant challenges without losing her own aloof personality fascinated me.

Next morning we drove to the place where we had left the

family and on arrival I hooted in the rhythm they now knew
well as the signal that we had brought their food. Soon, two
fully grown cheetah and three cubs came rushing towards us,
the cubs remained near the car while the others continued at
top speed to a lugga 400 yards away where they disappeared
in the undergrowth. I soon realized that what I had seen was
Pippa chasing Mbili, even though we were right in Mbili's
territory. She must have heard the familiar hooting signal
and come trustfully along, only to collide with Mbili, who
now treated her as a rival. This seemed to prove the theory
that it is common amongst cheetah for the mother to take over
the territory of a previous cub. I was sorry for Mbili and
could only hope that once the weather had improved, her
mother would return to her own hunting-grounds.

After Pippa had come back, panting from her successful
chase, we fed the family on the remains of their Grant kill.
Again I found it interesting that today, Somba did not object
to my holding out the meat for her, which obviously she no
longer regarded as a natural 'kill' for it was cut up and no
longer fresh.

Then we tried to trace Mbili's spoor but had no luck on the
muddy ground along the lugga. We had named it Hans Lugga,
after one of George's assistants who had once had to spend
the night there inside his small car when he got bogged crossing the lugga. He had been besieged all night by a pride of
lions, as well as stung by myriads of mosquitoes and, on top
of all this, had to walk at daybreak the five miles to Leopard
Rock to get help to pull the car out of the lugga.

Water only ran in the Hans Lugga during the rains, but
small puddles remained throughout the year and were the
only water supply between the Murera and Mulika rivers,
which ran parallel to each other at a distance of seven miles.
Since the plains on either side of the lugga were at present the
only comparatively dry ground in the surrounding marshes,
many animals congregated here, including predators who
found good cover along the lugga's undergrowth. I could only

pray and rely on Pippa's cleverness to keep her cubs out of trouble.

Later in the afternoon I had to drive to Leopard Rock and on the way saw Mbili on a termite hill within half a mile of the place at which she had disappeared in the morning. She watched me calmly as I walked up to her and only when I came within touching distance did she snarl, and even then she did not stir. I chatted in a low voice and in the way I had often talked to her in the past and walked round to see if she were pregnant, but I could not judge this while she was lying down. It was now nine months since she had lived alone, and four months (except for our meeting a few days ago) since I had last seen her. What more could I ask than that she still trusted me and treated me as a friend, even though I was of no immediate use to her?

The rain now increased so heavily that driving became impossible. One late afternoon, returning from the cheetah, we were crossing the flooded Mulika when in the middle of the raging torrent there was a splutter, and the engine stopped. The water was rising rapidly, and in spite of being drenched to the bone we sweated for two hours as we pushed the Land-Rover inch by inch on to the road; by then it was pitch dark . . . Two lions had been roaring uncomfortably near, and had probably been amused watching us.

The poor cheetah had more than their share of the rains and were hardly ever dry. Consequently they were often in an irritable mood. We watched them many times during the cloud-burst, huddling together and keeping their backs against the storm. But as soon as the worst was over the cubs quickly regained their playful spirit and, chasing each other through the water-puddles, also gave us a good splash. After another night of non-stop rain we met the family within half a mile of the camp. To get there they must have crossed the flooded, crocodile-infested Vasorongi. How they had done this I could not imagine as the rivulet was now far too wide to jump across, and even we, when wading through it earlier, waist-deep and hanging on to branches, had almost been swept away by the strong current and had had to turn back.

I could not understand why Pippa made no effort to come into camp, where she knew there was meat, but instead sat put where we met her until she turned in the opposite direction to hunt for herself. A few days later we found her again near the Hans Lugga, stalking a Grant's gazelle during a heavy downpour. After an unsuccessful chase she settled on one of the few patches of high ground surrounded by three inches of water. It had taken us four hours, plodding and slithering across the muddy six miles with our heavy loads, to reach the place, but I wanted to make sure that the family would not starve during these trying weeks.

After they had devoured the meat the cubs climbed up a slippery tree, Tiny excelling himself as usual. He often spent a long time on these lofty look-outs, partly to keep his feet dry and partly to search for prey. Somba was also very good at spotting anything moving, and only Big Boy was too lazy to exert himself, but he was the most good-natured of them all. Poor Pippa was now often unlike herself and grumpy from fatigue due to trying to hunt and to keep her cubs safe. Her frequent yawns showed how worn out she was, and she was much too tired to play with her children.

But not only cheetah had a tough time during these deluges. Once we were led by vultures to a newly born buffalo calf lying in four-inch-deep water: it must have been born during a storm and drowned. All animal life was changed by the floods. Never before had I realized that even scorpions could swim until we watched one paddling through a puddle. Instead of the never-failing francolins, which were normally far more numerous here than anywhere else, there were now large flocks of European stork and maribou, picking up tadpoles and frogs from the marshes. Even the porcupines abandoned their safe hiding-places and we surprised a pair under a rocky ledge, far too narrow to protect them from an enemy although they tried their best to frighten us by rattling their quills. Not to my comfort, I found myself hostess to a red spitting cobra who tried to keep dry behind the door of my dining-hut, where I found her coiled up when I wanted to close the door. She remained there persistently for three days, in spite of all my efforts to poke her out with a long stick without letting her spit venom into my eyes.

But far more upsetting was the fact that my cook, having by now had enough of the rains, bolted. I could not blame him since the Vasorongi, which normally runs six feet below my camp, was now level with it, and only did not flood the huts, as it had done during the previous rains, because the men had cleared its banks of the thick vegetation which had then held up the water. With no transport it was difficult to get a new cook and I had to waste precious time keeping camp life going. This was especially tiresome as it now took us most of the day to cover the seven miles to help the cheetah on the Hans plains. Our small herd of goats, installed at the abandoned Kenmare Lodge, was dwindling rapidly, and we could not afford to risk the meat going bad in the humid weather if we carried it all day and did not find the family. So I often therefore went ahead with Local to look for them, and he then returned to the camp to pick up the meat and to collect Stanley to help carry it.

5. Pippa meets Mbili again

One morning, when crossing the Mulika at 'Mile 5' on our
way to the family, we heard the agitated chatter of vervet
monkeys. Soon after we saw a cheetah head peeping through
the grass some hundred yards off the road. It was Mbili on
the boundary of her territory. Fearing that she might be
starving owing to the heavy rains, I took a leg of goat, walked
within two yards of her and dropped it. She quickly carried
it to a nearby tree to which I followed her and then watched
her eating the meat to the last scrap. She proved to be quite
an expert at crunching even the leg bones of a goat, and by
that I could judge how hungry she had been. She was in
excellent condition, and her coat was now so dark that I had
mistaken her at the first glance for Tatu. To be able always
to identify Pippa's families I had taken photographs of the
rumps of all her cubs to show the spots at the root of their tails
where they often grew into a solid line of up to eight spots.
Although this pattern varied individually it never changed,
and by these I knew I could recognize each cub even years
later when their faces and habits might have altered.

We then continued to the Hans plains a mile away where
we found Pippa. The family were playing happily in the sun,
which was a rare treat in the now usually overcast weather.
After all had eaten I collected every scrap they left behind in
case we should meet Mbili again and she might be in cub.

When nearing the place where we had left her earlier, I
called, and in response a cheetah head appeared above the
grass about 500 yards away. Local and I approached
cautiously, only to notice another cheetah next to it – they
were Tatu and Whity. Tatu charged instantly until I dropped
the meat scraps which kept her busy for the time being. When

Whity went to join her I saw that she was pregnant and ready to drop her cubs at any moment. Suddenly, I detected a third cheetah racing along, and – prr prr prr – Mbili seemed overjoyed to meet her sisters. She only got a friendly welcome from Tatu, both licking and purring and dancing around each other. Whity kept her distance and growled fiercely whenever Mbili tried to get near her. But she was not to be so easily put off, and did her best to disarm Whity – miaowing softly and rolling invitingly on to her back, only to get another rebuke in response. As much as Mbili was determined to win her sister over, so much was Whity determined to shoo her off. In the process of trying to outwit each other both moved gradually some hundred yards away to a tree where Whity settled herself, panting. It was touching to watch Mbili using all her shrewdness and tact, creeping nearer inch by inch, until she too sat down. During these manœuvres Tatu had made the best of the meagre remains of the scraps, and now she too rested at a short distance.

During all this time Local and I had remained absolutely still, then, seeing the sisters settling down, we retreated slowly backwards towards the road, hoping they would soon make friends. But Mbili followed us until we crossed the Mulika and were out of her territory.

All three sisters were now within Mbili's territory, so too was Pippa, who was only separated from her previous litter by the flooded Hans Lugga about a quarter of a mile away. The last time I had been together with the three cubs of the earlier litter was nine months and twenty days ago near the Murera gate, about fourteen miles from here. Since then Whity and Tatu had been seen together on several occasions around Mugwongo Hill, some twelve miles away in the opposite direction. Mbili had always remained alone between 'Mile 5' and Leopard Rock. All three were now much larger than their mother and superbly fit.

I was convinced, not only from her appearance, but also by her behaviour in resenting Mbili's approaches so vehemently, that Whity would give birth within forty-eight hours. Knowing that the three sisters could well look after themselves even during these trying rains, I told Local and Stanley that we would not feed them unless we should find Whity with her future cubs in desperate need of help, otherwise we might annul all they had achieved in becoming wild.

But having once given Mbili meat, she was waiting for us the next morning at 'Mile 5'. I felt very unhappy at having, in her own interest, to harden my heart. Ignoring her I walked on. But I had not reckoned with Local and Stanley who, contrary to my instructions, called Mbili, with the result that she followed us. They did not understand that I only acted as I did to prevent a possible fight between Mbili and Pippa. I used every kind of trick and device to evade Mbili who trotted trustfully along beside us. However, eventually she disappeared and we continued for another mile. As soon as I detected the family through field-glasses some 500 yards away, we inserted the vitamin rations into small pieces of meat to have all ready when they arrived. While thus preoccupied I had not noticed that Mbili caught up with us and was now sitting within a few yards, watching us intently.

Meanwhile Pippa and the cubs had come close but, on seeing Mbili, bolted instantly. This surprised me, but only proved again how little I knew Pippa, because she had only run away to lead the cubs into safety. Now she returned to deal with Mbili. Growling threateningly, she crouched, her head lower than her shoulders, staring at her with deadly purposefulness while Mbili reacted in this same way. Desperately I tried to prevent a fight, which I was in no doubt would be won by Mbili as she was physically at an advantage being bigger than Pippa, as well as morally at an advantage in defending her territory. All my efforts to interfere were in vain and the cheetah reached each other. Then, just when Pippa was ready to spring, Mbili suddenly rolled on to her back and, uttering a soft moan, surrendered. Instantly Pippa left her and went to a tree under which I had stored the tripe and intestines. Normally she did not touch viscera but now she gobbled them up while Mbili watched her from about ten yards away. Meanwhile I quickly rescued the meat cutlets containing the vitamin rations to save them for the cubs, so that they might at least eat these. To my amazement Pippa now joined the cubs, whom during the encounter she had 'ordered' to sit still some hundred yards away. Now she waited with them for me to bring the meat we had secured inside a basket hanging on the branch of a tree. While they were tucking in Mbili finished off the scraps Pippa had left, and then moved quietly towards a herd of Grant that had appeared far away.

I took a deep breath. Thank God it looked as if there wouldn't be a fight, but I wondered if this was only a truce or if I had witnessed the final parting of Pippa and Mbili. I knew that lion and wolves surrender to the victor in their fights for leadership – the wolf rolling on its back and exposing its throat as the most vulnerable part of its body, and the lion offering its belly. In both cases the victor never takes advantage of this surrender but is satisfied that his opponent has admitted defeat. I never realized until now that a similar code of honour existed between mother and daughter cheetah where neither leadership nor the well-known submission of a cub to its mother could be the reason for the fight. What I had seen seemed to me to illustrate the innate law that a child cannot take action against its parent however much – as in this case – it might be morally in the right when justifiably defending its territory, and also be physically the stronger. Unfortunately, where human beings transgress this law, homicide may take place, but surely one has to regard this as a perversion of natural law. Of course one might argue that Mbili only submitted because she sensed that Pippa would defend her tiny cubs much more vigorously than she would normally fight a rival; but this argument might well be invalid as Mbili could be pregnant, as Whity was, and thus have a double reason – maternal and territorial defence – to motivate her actions.

However one may be inclined to interpret Mbili's behaviour, it is interesting to note that for the next few days we never found her spoor nearer than a few hundred yards from Pippa, and that a labour-gang later saw her several times along the road within a mile from the place where they had had their contest.

Pippa remained in Mbili's territory on the Hans plain, which was the driest ground in the area and therefore attracted many animals. Once we found her stalking a herd of twenty-six oryx with a small calf; another time she tried her luck at stalking a Grant fawn, but in both cases she was chased off by the mothers. It was becoming increasingly difficult to keep up the number of our goats, and so we were almost glad when George discovered a giraffe, bogged down in liquid mud, which must have died shortly before he found her. Although giraffe is not on their natural menu all the cheetah liked the meat and waited every morning at a specific tree for this new treat.

One day we found Pippa alone and I sensed trouble. When after some time she called prr prr and the cubs showed up, I noticed that Somba walked in a peculiar way, nosing the ground and listening to the grass when the others brushed against it. When she came near enough for me I saw that both her eyes were closed and very swollen. The underlids were darkly discoloured, the eyes were covered by a fleshy mucus reminiscent of a nictitating membrane, except for a tiny spot at the outer corner of the right one. Poor Somba walked like the blind, following scent and sound since I could see no other injury. I assumed that a cobra had spat into her eyes. I gave her as much meat as she could hold, which she took willingly from my hand. Later she even tried to join the other cubs in their games, but soon lay down with both eyes closed. As if to make things still more complicated, I now spotted Mbili a few hundred yards away along the road. Luckily a few moments later a Land-Rover approached and Mbili vanished. Recognizing the Warden I signalled him to stop and told him of poor Somba's mishap. He suggested bathing her eyes with a weak solution of permanganate which I had at the camp; so we walked home to get it and when we returned at teatime, we saw the spoor of Mbili near 'Mile 5'. Relieved that she was now about two miles from Pippa, we continued to the Hans plain; here we found the family where we had left them. I had brought a fair amount of the solution and cotton wool, prepared to spill most of it in the attempt to treat Somba. As soon as I came near her she turned into a raging fury, striking blindly at me. So I waited until she was occupied drinking milk then I quickly dabbed the soaked cotton wool on to her eyes, the permanganate ran all down her face. During the next four days I repeated this as often as I had the chance. By then her eyes were almost normal and the little devil could now see where to bring her strokes 'home'. At least I could judge by her defence that she was fit again, and I was very glad that the tranquillizer and airbag that I had brought to carry her to my camp in case I might have to treat her inside the reinforced enclosure never had to be used.

I had a great deal of sympathy for Somba, but this did not go as far as wanting to share her experience with the cobra. This very nearly happened when I asked Local to repair the wooden board which covered the bathroom annexe of my sleeping-hut. He returned very quickly, showing me a milky substance sprayed over his shin, the venom of a spitting cobra. He had found her when lifting up the floorboards, and in the second it took him to let the board fall back on her, she spat, but luckily from her precarious position missed his eyes (nevertheless, the skin on which the venom landed must have been abrased for it came off, and left pigmentless scars all over his leg). We now approached the board most cautiously, and sure enough, in the dim light beneath I saw a grey cobra as thick as my arm coiled in a solid heap. I hesitated to poke her out since I had nothing with which to kill such a large snake, and she might charge and strike, so we decided to walk over to the Warden and ask for his help. We had not gone far when he drove up in his four-wheel drive Volvo, the only vehicle powerful enough to use on the muddy roads. It was surprising that the cobra had not moved away since Local had discovered her and slammed the wooden board on her; she was still in the same place when the Warden fired his rifle into the heap of coiled cobra. It was a monster – seven feet four inches long. The longest spitting cobra whose measurements have been authentically recorded was over nine feet. However, this one was good enough for me not to want to share the bathroom with it, and by the many depressions we found beneath the board she must have resided there for some time.

Another reptile who shared my bedroom was a female agama, a foot long and dull brown, shabby compared to the male's striking turquoise-coloured body and bright orange head. Several of these harmless lizards lived in my camp and this particular female almost developed into a pet and slept for many weeks in the groove below the door bolt; she never minded if I touched her when I used the bolt.

Side by side with the agamas lived the little geckos who used the palm log walls as nurseries and laid their eggs inside convenient holes where they were safe from rain and enemies. These harmless creatures were very tame, especially after dark when I turned on the gas-lamp which attracted many insects. Then they waited in ambush to catch one insect after the other with lightning speed, never getting so close to the hot lamp as to burn themselves.

Whilst writing about cold-blooded creatures I must record that I never realized how useful frogs could be to predators until I watched Pippa. She had now been two weeks on the Hans plains and one morning she and I were listening attentively to the croaking of the frogs along the lugga a few hundred yards away, when suddenly their chorus stopped. Pippa called prr prr, and instantly the family was off. Later we found the fresh spoor of lion leading towards the lugga; this had obviously upset the frogs who, by their sudden silence, had warned Pippa of danger.

Pippa

opposite
Pippa carrying a c[...]
28 days old

Eating meat,
5 weeks old

The fourth litter
at 17 days and
at 27 days *below*

Learning to climb, 7 weeks old

The cub killed by a lion

The cubs, 8 weeks old, playing with Pippa

Pippa and her family, 9 weeks old, on the Mulika termite hill

The little cub wanted to be reassured

The cubs playing

Pippa and the 3 months old cubs on a Grant kill

Somba 'defending' it

By now the weather had improved and Pippa found an ideal terminalia tree within a mile of the Mulika which she chose as our rendezvous. Whenever we arrived and called, it did not take long for the family to appear if they were hungry. Twice they did not turn up, but following circling vultures, we were guided to Pippa who had just killed a young Grant. On both occasions we found her sitting at a short distance watching the cubs play with the carcass for so long that I was sure she wanted them to learn how to open it up. Somba was very busy defending the kill, and frightening Tiny off; so there was only Big Boy left, who finally got the idea and, chewing off the tail, thus found an opening through which to tear out the intestines. Only then did Pippa join in the meal.

It was Christmas again, and it coincided with the presence of fledglings of the fifth generation of wiretails inside my studio hut. These friendly swallows trusted me absolutely and did not mind my frequent movements right below the nest which they had built against the roofing rafts. Within five feet of it I had secured a stick for them to perch on; on this the parent birds were now sitting, calling their chick to leave the nest. But the fledgling did not dare to venture beyond the rim, and, balancing unsteadily, seemed too terrified to move however encouragingly the parents chirped. Finally they flew out of the hut, thus trying to tempt the chick into following, and sure enough, it now took a great plunge and parachuted to the perch, hanging on to it for dear life. Instantly the parents reappeared and sat to the right and left of their frightened offspring, chirping most excitedly. All this happened not more than two yards away from where I was writing letters. I love this happy family who had now lived for two years with us, and obviously accepted us as harmless.

After this successful experiment I prepared our Christmas Tree. I had selected a small balanites tree and on its long thorns I hung up an international assortment of Christmas decorations which I had collected over our camping years, many of which had been sent by friends from all over the world; with the addition of tinsel the tree finally looked rather attractive. This year I had a special surprise for my staff – a Swahili version of the carol 'Silent Night, Holy Night'. The Austrian Embassy had presented me with a record of this carol which they had translated for the Africans to celebrate the 150th Anniversary of the composition of this famous Austrian carol. So after I had lit the candles and given the men their usual gifts of cigarettes, sweets and money, we played the carol on a record-player which George had given me as a Christmas present. It was most touching to watch the men listening, their eyes getting bigger and softer, as they were moved by the music. For me, a born Austrian, it meant a great deal to see the effect it had on these three primitive Africans out in the bush. I had often wondered whether if only one were to play 'Silent Night, Holy Night' before troops all tensed up by fear and terror before going into battle, the magic of the tune might perhaps at this very last moment prevent man from killing man.

It was the first time for many years that George and I had been alone on Christmas Eve, and after the candles had burnt down we sat in the dark looking at the myriads of sparkling stars and listening to the meaningful stillness around us. My mind turned to the Christmas Eves of people living under conditions as different as possible from ours – where neon lights and fire-crackers illuminated the dark night and loud-speakers ceaselessly blared out carols, competing with the drumming of the traffic. I thought of the many problems we humans have become involved in since we began to live by our 'man-made values', which differ so utterly from the fundamental values that nature has evolved over millions of years. How could a city-dweller, trapped in air-conditioned rooms between chasms of concrete skyscrapers, where fresh air and privacy have become the greatest luxuries, understand values which are based on the co-operation of all living things – ecology? If he bases his need for security on his bank account, aims for status symbol with material possessions, and invents synthetic substitutes for food and medicines, how can he still know the timeless laws of nature which have kept life pulsing on our planet for far longer than we can grasp? If he over-values his ego and uses his superior intellect to destroy, can he believe that we are only a small part of 'living matter' created for keeping up the balance of nature?

The longer I live close to wild animals, the more I believe that we can learn a lot from them – indeed have to learn from them – if we want to survive. We need to know how they solve the problem of territorial rights; how they complement their food supplies (under natural conditions, the various food preferences and requirements keep the vegetation in balance and the soil fertile); how they cope with birth control;* how they discipline their children, without being possessive; and how they communicate with each other for the purpose of understanding rather than to interfere.

My thoughts were interrupted by faint lion roars which brought me quickly back to our own problems. One of these was how to increase interest in the conservation of wild life. The Elsa Wild Animal Appeal headquarters in England had, since it was launched in 1961, carried out important projects. As it was primarily dependent on the royalties I earned from books and films, I realized that I had to find a way for it to carry on when those royalties ceased. Therefore, three years ago, I established the Elsa Wild Animal Appeal in the USA in the hope of not only raising funds but also of educating the younger generation to take an active part in conservation work. Both organizations were charities and consequently tax-exempt.

Today we were concerned to win over the younger generation of Africans so that they would protect the local animals, which depend on their help more than on that of anybody else. This plan had started operating seven months ago, a short time before Pippa gave birth to her present cubs. Taking
* The lion and cheetah mothers will not mate during the period their young are dependent on their help.

advantage of her pregnancy, after which I would have to remain near her all the time to keep her supplied with food, I had taken a friend to the Samburu Game Reserve. There I met a group of African students who had won a prize for writing essays on wildlife; the prize was a free visit to this Park. At the request of the Warden I gave an informal talk to the group, after which they volunteered to start a Wildlife Club for Africans. Since then these students had visited my camp with their teachers to discuss further developments of their plans. In consequence a seminar, lasting three days, was organized with the result that the Government agreed to sponsor the initiation of Kenyan Wildlife Clubs – while the African Wildlife Leadership Foundation, the East African Wildlife Society and the Elsa Appeal would share the cost of the clubs' administration. We were very glad to help in financing this worthy cause, especially as it had been generated entirely by Africans who wanted to involve schools and youth organizations in helping to preserve wild animals. Now we had to see that they kept up their enthusiasm.

This was all very good, but for me my immediate duty was to learn more about wild animals while I had such unique opportunities for doing this.

The day after, we found the family in drizzling rain on the plain near 'Mile 5'. Pippa was very nervous and craned her neck continuously to look above the high grass. Unfortunately the ground was much too wet for finding spoor which might have explained the cause of her anxiety. The following morning she was again extremely irritable, and after gulping down the meat took her cubs far off into the plain. Soon afterwards, we found the spoor of two lions on the road. Suddenly I had an uncanny feeling of being watched, and the next moment Local gripped me by the shoulder, whispering that there were two lions in a bush right on the road. The moment we stopped, they got up and looked at us, and I recognized Boy and Suswa, two lions belonging to George's pride. They now moved slowly off in the opposite direction from that which

Pippa had taken. They must have found it difficult to hunt in the wet weather around the Mugwongo swamp, which had been their home for two years, and were obviously looking for new hunting-fields. Their presence made it very difficult for us to search for Pippa as they not only knew my hooting signal, which I also used when visiting George, but might be attracted by the scent of the meat we carried for the cheetah, and follow us to her. On our return to camp we learned that Ugas had called during our absence; luckily he had left his two companions, a wild lion and lioness, at a short distance while he inspected our huts.

Now I could fully understand Pippa's apprehension when finding herself surrounded by so many lions but, because of the still marshy state of the plains adjoining her present domain, she had no choice but to remain within the limited area where we had recently found her. Poor Pippa – next morning she was still close to where we had left her, and still tense – so obviously some lion was still around. After we had fed the family, we followed them to a small termite hill from which they could look around – but could also be seen. Leaving them there we moved on for about a hundred yards, when suddenly a lion's head rose from the high grass not more than ten yards from us. Terrified, I stopped, until I recognized Ugas. He looked at me with his one eye* as if it was the most natural thing for us to meet here, and after a few minutes sank back again into the grass. Only then did I feel my heart begin to beat again. Although we now knew the exact spot where Ugas was, we could see nothing which might betray the presence of such a large animal.

Hoping that his belly was too full for him to take interest in cheetah cubs, we led our family some 500 yards away, which was as far as they would move. Next morning heavy fog enveloped the Park; it was so thick that we could not see farther than a few yards. I had never experienced such fog in
* The other had to be removed some time previously owing to an injury.

all the ten years I had been camping here on and off, and only
hoped that Pippa was all right. My worries increased when we
saw cheetah and lion spoor mixed up together on the road
leading to the Hans Lugga. There we found the family, complete and happy on a termite hill close to the road, where
recently a labour-gang had dug deep ditches to drain off the
water. These ditches were connected by a cement culvert laid
three feet underground across the road. As soon as the mist
cleared up the culvert became the cubs' playground. They
chased each other in and out of the big tunnel, one waiting at
the far end to ambush, another emerging from the dark hole
or bouncing from the top on to it; they had heavenly fun. I
was surprised to watch this new game, so contrary to cheetah
nature for they always make sure of a safe retreat; perhaps
the cubs were so relaxed because they knew that Pippa was
sitting close by and while they were trapped inside the long
culvert would watch out for any possible danger.

When tired of the tunnel game they moved on to the
murram stacks which lined the road nearby. Jumping up the
loose gravel was not too easy and the cubs often rolled back
before reaching the top. But once one of them was 'King of
the Murram Stack', it defended its position savagely if a
rival dared to undermine it or pull it off by the tail. Those
stacks were also grand for playing hide-and-seek, in which
Pippa often joined. It was most amusing to watch the family
careering at incredible speed between these stacks until all
were exhausted and rested, panting, under a large terminalia
tree which grew most conveniently right on the road and provided not only shade but also a good look-out from its lower
branches. I settled myself close to Pippa and, caressing her
silky fur, listened to her purring. After a little while I also
felt drowsy and placed my head in a comfortable position
between her front leg and ribs and, feeling her body heaving
rhythmically with her breathing, dozed off.

The family liked this place so much that they remained here
for many days until the roadworks were resumed. Then they

moved about a mile away to a tree with a large bent-down branch which gave me splendid opportunities to photograph the cheetah 'sitting silhouetted against the sky, or competing for the best position. We called the tree 'Photo Tree' since for several weeks, it became a favourite rendezvous. I had recently acquired a Norelco (Philips) tape-recorder, light enough to carry in addition to my Leica, Bolex cine camera and field-glasses. Holding the microphone within a few inches of the cheetah did not upset them, and so I was able to record most of their sound variations quite clearly. One of the few I could not get on to tape was Somba's 'Wa Wa Wa' which she had uttered on rare occasions when defending her food. She had lately become quite unpredictable and could at one moment be surprisingly friendly, only to change at the next without the slightest provocation. Watching Pippa on these occasions made me love and respect her more and more, and only wished that all human beings had as much patience and tact in coping with difficult children as this animal mother had.

On our daily walks to the cheetah we had watched an ostrich family since the chicks had hatched three months ago. Out of the original thirteen only five were now alive. The tiny chicks were easy prey, and we had actually seen an eagle swooping down to pick one up before the parents were aware of its presence. (Pippa could not tackle a fully grown ostrich, but had killed a few half-grown ones in the past.)

On the day that the cubs were twenty-four weeks and five days old I squeezed out the last drop of milk from Pippa's teats. Comparing this period with the fourteen weeks after which her milk had dried up with her second litter, I wondered if the present prolonged lactation might be due to the daily doses of calcium I had given her while she was nursing these cubs.

Up to now I had rigidly adhered to my rule of not letting strangers come near the cheetah, however lonely I might feel deprived of all human company. During the tourist season it was trying to watch the cars by-passing my camp because the word had gone around that I was not co-operative. Being no hermit by nature it was sometimes very hard to stick to my principle, but it paid off as Pippa's family was already much shyer than many of the wild cheetah in other National Parks which frequently jumped on to vehicles. Of course I could not prevent visitors stopping their cars to watch the family if they spotted them in the bush, for they came here to see the animals, but it made all the difference if I were there to introduce the strangers to the cheetah and thus encourage them to accept them as part of our family. As long as I reserved this privilege to Local, Stanley and myself, there would be no danger of spoiling their wild instincts once we withdrew.

But now, three times within a fortnight I was confronted with the need to break my rule, which, after careful consideration, I felt justified in doing. The first occasion was when Frank Minot visited the Park; he had originally helped me to adopt Pippa and, as he had not seen her since she had given birth to her cubs, I took him to the family whom he watched from inside his car. So also did Lady William Percy, who had shown great interest in Elsa and Pippa since they had entered my life; and thirdly my publisher, Billy Collins, wanted to see the family before bringing out the book *The Spotted Sphinx* in a few months' time. Although my friends used great tact not to upset the family I was only too well aware that they were only tolerated because I acted as a liaison between all of us.

On the 18th of January I received a letter from the Director of Kenya National Parks, offering me two leopard cubs for rehabilitation in the Meru Park as he knew how keen I was to study leopards and to compare them with lion and cheetah. Overjoyed, I accepted because I believed that Pippa would avoid my camp with her present litter, as she had done up to now, and I could keep the leopard cubs inside Whity's enclosure for the time being.

6. An Accident and its Consequences

On the 22nd of January, I drove to Nairobi in convoy with John Baxendale, who was helping George with the lions. I went ahead in my new six-cylinder Land-Rover with one of George's staff in the back. I had covered half the distance when, climbing up a long hill where the road was freshly mur-ramed and cut along the sides of a steep slope, which ended in a river far below, I came around a bend and saw two Africans walking in the middle of the road a few hundred yards ahead. There was plenty of time for them to respond to my hooting, but they ignored it and walked on hand in hand until I had no choice but to drive the car near to the escarpment edge in order to avoid them. Here the gravel was still very loose and the car skidded and hit a milestone. The next thing I knew was that I was lying halfway down the escarpment in a mass of broken glass a few yards from the smashed-up car. My first thought was about the African. After I had called his name, I saw him struggling from the car, thank God with no worse injury than a scratch on his forehead. This was incredibly lucky, as the car had overturned and was facing in the opposite direction from which we had come; it must have somersaulted whilst plunging down the slope. Still more lucky was that it had been held up by a few bushes halfway down; otherwise we would have rolled right into the river at the bottom. I now tried to get up but found it difficult because of the pain, which seemed to go all through me, also my right hand was a mess of blood and earth. Helped by the African, I clambered up the eighty yards to the road and sat down. My hand was bleeding heavily, and I could only bear the pain by holding it upright. After a while a bus appeared, carrying amongst the African passengers the local chief. Kindly he poured some iodine from his first-aid kit on to my hand. I felt no reaction to the normal burning sensation of the disinfectant. This made me fear the worst. The Chief offered to take us to the nearest dispensary. While I was being helped into the bus John Baxendale caught up with us. Taking in the situation at a glance, he arranged with the Chief for a guard to look after the car until the police could investigate the accident. Then he drove us to the provincial headquarters at Embu, eighty miles away, which we had to pass on our way to Nairobi. I was most grateful to John for carefully avoiding all the bumps on the bad road and yet trying to go as fast as possible because I could not stop the bleeding of my hand which left puddles of blood everywhere.

At the African Hospital in Embu, the dresser gave me an injection against tetanus, some pain-killing tablets, and a blanket to keep me warm and stop my teeth from chattering with shock. He then assured me that my African passenger had only superficial scratches and could go home the next day. After providing him with money to buy food and his return ticket we left him, and went on for another eighty miles to Nairobi. By 9 p.m. when we reached the hospital, six hours had elapsed since the accident and I was in a bad state. It was most fortunate that my old friend and surgeon, Mr Gerald Nevill, was available to do the operation immediately; it took three hours. Although my body was one bruise and all the colours of the spectrum, I had no serious injury other than that to my right hand. The skin on the back of the hand was gone, all the tendons were severed and all the bones had been knocked about half an inch out of alignment.

For the time being, all that could be done was to place a skin graft over the hand. When this had healed, new tendons would need to be transplanted from my leg to my hand, which would mean another operation in about six months' time. During the following month in hospital, I had plenty of time to reflect on how lucky I had been to survive this accident and I thought of this whenever I felt depressed at knowing that it would take at least two years and several operations before I might perhaps recover the use of my right hand.

Of course there was now no question of taking over the two leopard cubs (which would be far too big for rehabilitation in a few months). My most urgent need was to find somebody to help me with the cheetah, as well as with more personal chores, such as dressing, bathing, cutting food, and the other things I could no longer do for myself. It was lucky for me that at this time a young American, Mary, arrived in Kenya, urgently wanting a job. Preferring to work with animals and live in the bush, she fitted in with my needs and, moreover, she could also type and drive a car. So we arranged for her to get a working permit which under these circumstances was granted to a non-Kenya citizen.

Meanwhile, George and John had taken it in turn to drive Local and Stanley the long distance to the cheetah who had remained for more than two weeks around the 'Photo Tree'. Then they had moved gradually nearer the camp, until they settled at the 'Kill Acacia' about half a mile across the river. This was the nearest Pippa had brought these cubs to the camp, although she had used the 'Kill Acacia' frequently with Mbili, Whity and Tatu. This tree had the great advantage that the cheetah could rest and feed under its shade without being seen by vultures, who by circling round might give them away to other predators. Also, the lower branches were an ideal lookout over the surrounding plain and the cheetah could easily spot a car arriving at my camp and thus keep clear of strangers.

The men saw the family, with one exception, daily, and so felt sure that Pippa had not killed during my absence.

When Mary and I returned on the 22nd of February, exactly one month after the accident, Pippa had taken the cubs earlier that morning to the road about a mile from camp. During the next few days she continued to move until she discovered a newly-dug murram quarry on the Vasorongi, five miles upstream. The Park Warden had recently decided to move the headquarters from Leopard Rock to a place not far from there, and needed murram to surface the new site. For the time being the roadworks had stopped, and so the cheetah were the 'Kings of the Large Pit' where they found an ideal playground in its many piles and trenches.

I felt apprehensive as to how the family would react to Mary, who was driving the car, and we decided that she should not leave the Land-Rover until they had got used to her presence. To make our reunion easier, we had brought along a complete sheep. Soon after I had hooted the familiar signal, the family appeared. Ignoring my white bandaged arm and foot, the cubs bounced on the carcass, while Pippa sat by watching them pulling and tearing at the skin in their efforts to open it. I sat next to her, caressing her while she purred and licked my hand. How often had I thought of doing just this while I had been in hospital. Now I felt so happy, knowing that she too was glad that we were together again. The cubs were in excellent form, despite having by now lost all their deciduous teeth. I could see that their permanent canines had grown two millimetres – they were now seven months and ten days old. During the teeth-changing period, they had great difficulty in chewing, let alone opening a carcass, and I felt very sorry for them as I watched them dancing frantically around the sheep and tackling it ceaselessly until after ten minutes Big Boy succeeded in tearing it open at the tail. Now Pippa thought it time to share the meal, and for the next two hours I listened to the squeals and gurgles of the cubs fighting over the meat, chewing and crunching up bones; I wondered why I loved these noises, as people's eating noises irritate me. Was it that animals eat only to sustain their lives, while our habit of using meals as a part of social entertainment at which rigid rules concerning table manners prevail forbids such noises?

I was glad to see that my long absence had not changed the

cubs' trust in me. Somba tried to charge, but after I said a
firm 'No', she settled down and even allowed me to dangle
intestines into her mouth. Big Boy needed no help and gobbled
up with gusto everything the others refused. Only Tiny still
required coaxing, and went without food rather than fight for
it.

Suddenly three ostrich appeared far off. Instantly the
cheetah all sat up, growled, and watched with hard eyes as
the birds continued walking slowly on their way. They only
began to eat again when one of them kept watch until the
ostrich disappeared. Soon after, I was startled by the jarring
engine vibrations of a tractor 500 yards away. To my surprise, the cheetah ignored this noise completely, just as they
never took any notice of an aircraft.

Mary had remained all morning at the driver's seat and,
after a short inspection by Pippa, seemed accepted. Next
morning there was no sign of the family. I felt rather relieved,
as we had run out of meat and I only had milk to offer them.
Later in the day I took three friends from the USA for a drive
in the Park. On our way we stopped once more at the murram
pit where we found the cheetah right in the open, apparently
waiting for us. My friends of course remained inside the car,
while I held out the milk bowl to the cubs, who in their
eagerness pushed all three heads in together and nearly spilled
the contents. It was especially difficult for me to hold the
bowl with my left hand only, and so I hoped that Mary
could soon make friends with the family and be able to help in
feeding them.

Next day I had a treat for the cheetah, the meat of a
buffalo which had been shot on control. It always puzzled me
why Pippa's families were so very fond of buffalo and zebra
meat, since both were animals which they would not have
been able to kill except if they were very young. But they became quite crazy when we gave them the meat and filled
themselves to bursting point. Somba especially ate more than
I believed she could hold, and was fiercely at loggerheads

with Pippa over the best titbits. Watching to see that nobody could get more than she, she still found time to charge me twice when I refilled the water container, though I stopped her with a 'No' each time. After she was unable to eat any more, she sat close to me, watching me intensely. We were no more than a few inches from each other; though I risked being ripped open, I stood her long and scrutinizing gaze which seemed to be a challenge as to which of us would be the future boss. I kept completely still, just looking at her, for a long, long time – until, in fact, she rolled over and relaxed. More than ever did I believe that Somba was only fierce when her territorial and food-defence instincts were aroused; once she realized that neither was threatened, she became as placid as her brothers. Big Boy could never be provoked and was incredibly tolerant and very self-assured; the two other cubs were rarely at loggerheads with him, though they often were with Pippa. But now the family was far too full with buffalo meat for any quarrels, and rested panting, with their heavy bellies in the air.

I thought this was a good opportunity for introducing Mary, and so signalled her to join us. Slowly she sat herself near me, while on my other side Pippa dozed. I patted Pippa, and gradually Mary did the same until Pippa was being stroked only by her. Somba watched with half-closed eyes, ready to defend her mother, but when she saw her so at ease, she too relaxed. We all had a peaceful sleep during the midday heat, until Pippa thought it time to move. Followed by Big Boy and Tiny, she walked slowly off with swinging belly, while Somba, who had eaten more than any of them, searched for still more meat until she found a chunk too big for her to grab, so straddled it away. Unbelievable as it appeared, she still seemed hungry the next day and followed me whenever I gave meat to the others to make sure she was not done out of her share. Otherwise, she was very friendly, never once attacked me, and seemed now to accept me as the 'boss'. Poor Tiny was off colour. Sitting with a very distended belly, he did not touch the food I offered him but instead chewed grass. I always watched the faeces (droppings) of the cheetah and so knew that none of them had worms, which might have been responsible for stomach trouble, so I assumed that Tiny had only indulged in too much buffalo meat, and this must have been the cause of his indisposition because the next day he was quite fit again.

No mother could have had three children more different in character and looks than Pippa had, and I was daily more impressed to observe how she made allowances for each without provoking jealousy or upsetting them. During the last few days she gradually moved back to the 'Photo Tree' where we found them on the following morning. Big Boy and Tiny seemed to have teething trouble and chewed bark or rubbed their gums against sticks, while Somba meanwhile made the best of the meat ration. Later, I photographed Tiny and Pippa sitting on a branch. Suddenly Tiny uttered a strange, deep-gurgling sound and the next moment all three cubs were off, bolting from a greater bustard which Tiny had spotted far away. Pippa watched this large bird without changing her position, and so reassured the cubs returned again to finish their meal.

A few days before, I had developed an infection on two toes which had been operated on while I was in hospital. Since I was unable to walk, Mary and the men went alone next day to the cheetah whom they found at the 'Photo Tree'. According to their reports, the family were feeding when Tiny again gave the alarm, and all ran off some fifty yards; then they stopped and watched Mbili approaching from the opposite direction. When she had come within a hundred yards of the car, Mbili kept hiding behind it, with the result that the family cleared off and never returned. So Local, obeying my instructions never to feed any of the previous cubs unless they were ill, collected the food remains and brought them back. As

I was not present to identify Mbili, I had to take Local's word that it had been Pippa who had given way today (the only explanation I could find for this was that the 'Photo Tree' was right inside Mbili's territory, and by now the ground was dry enough for Pippa to clear out of it).

In the afternoon, a party of visitors called at my camp amongst whom was a doctor. I consulted him about my toes, and he advised me to get them treated at the hospital as soon as possible. It was fortunate that the Warden had to fly next day to Nairobi and so I could get a lift which would save me the nine hours' trip by car; but I was less fortunate in being kept at the hospital for two weeks.

From the diary notes Mary wrote during my absence, I learned that the family remained for another ten days around the 'Photo Tree'. They allowed Mary to hold the milk bowl while they pushed their heads in all at once, but it took a week before they really made friends. Pippa was the first to come to Mary, and lie down at her feet, purring loudly while Mary stroked her.

Meanwhile, Somba was busy charging Stanley, trying to prevent him from removing the empty meat basket; hooking her teeth into it, they had a tug-of-war until she gave up and also came near Mary; after examining her carefully, especially her hands, she settled close and thus encouraged Tiny to investigate too. He had been quick to realize that I was not there to hand-feed him, so he had been fiercely at loggerheads with anybody who dared to take his meat, and became so efficient in defending it that even Somba treated him with respect. One morning only Pippa turned up at the 'Photo Tree'; after a while she called the cubs with a low moan, but when she got no response, guided Mary and the two men for half a mile to the Mulika, climbing two more trees on the way to call the cubs; finally they found them across the rivulet. Then the party of seven walked back to the meat which was locked inside the car.

All went well for ten days, until one early morning when

Mary drove the Land-Rover to the 'Photo Tree'. As soon as Local stepped out, two lionesses rose from the high grass about fifty yards away but, being wild, ran off quickly. Needless to say, the family had left the area and could not be found for five days.

7. Growing Up

I returned during their absence and learned that a few days before, on the 9th of March, Boy had mauled the Warden's child. Boy was one of George's lions; he and his sister, Girl had acted major parts in our film *Born Free*. As soon as filming had been completed, they were presented by their owners to George to rehabilitate them to the wild. Later they were joined by Ugas, and finally by four cubs – a lion and three lionesses. Despite the difference in their ages and background, all had amalgamated into one pride, though Boy and Girl kept very much together and had recently produced two cubs. Having been used to human company since they were very young, they were the most friendly of the pride.

The recent incident had taken place within a few hundred yards of the 'Photo Tree'. John Baxendale had found Boy on the road and, in the hope of bringing him back to George's camp twelve miles away, had allowed him to jump up on the roof of his Land-Rover and had then continued his journey. They were met by the Warden, travelling in the opposite direction with his wife and two small children in the front seat of an open-sided car. The Warden stopped within a few feet of John's car and got out to have a chat. While they were talking, Boy got down from the roof of the Land-Rover and slowly approached the Warden's car. Thinking that he contemplated jumping on to his car, the Warden got into the driving seat with the intention of moving on. By this time Boy was alongside, and suddenly rearing up leaned across the Warden and seized the arm of the four-year-old boy, who was sitting between his parents. At this moment the car, which was already in gear, started and lurched forward, dragging Boy along, walking on his hind legs, until he let go of the child's arm. Meanwhile the Warden was punching Boy with his fist, and the mother held on to her son and baby daughter on her lap. At no time did Boy show any sign of anger, as he certainly would have done at being thwarted of his prey, had he regarded the child as such. Although Boy's teeth had sunk deep into the child's upper arm, there was no muscle torn and no bones broken. Being late on Sunday afternoon there was unfortunately no aircraft available to fly the child to Nairobi Hospital. His father therefore took him by car to a Mission Hospital, an hour's drive up in the Nyambeni hills, where the child's wounds were dressed and sewn up; this was a great error, as wounds inflicted by a predator should never be completely closed but kept open to drain. By the following morning the boy's arm was in a bad state, and the first act of the doctor who arrived by air, was to re-open the wounds. To everyone's great relief the child recovered completely after six weeks in a Nairobi hospital.

The incident aroused great controversy and publicity. The Government ruled that Boy could remain in the Meru Park on the condition that George should from now on refrain from entertaining visitors with any of his lions, and should stop feeding them. Luckily, by now they could all look after themselves.

About this time a detailed programme of how I was to be allowed to carry on my work with the cheetah was drawn up; this was in addition to our mutual agreement made long ago which stated that I would terminate their rehabilitation by the end of this year. By that time the cubs would be seventeen and a half months old – the same age that Pippa's previous litter had been when she abandoned them. Now, as from the 1st of October, the goats had to be removed from Kenmare and kept outside the Park, and the feeding of the cheetah was to be gradually reduced until the 1st of December, when it was to stop.

When George and I had started rehabilitating our animals here four years ago, we had built our camps twelve miles apart, assuming this to be far enough to keep the lions and cheetah out of each other's territories. But recently the lions had come more frequently into Pippa's area, which naturally interfered with her movements. So I was startled when the family appeared one midday right in my camp, for the first time since the cubs were born eight months earlier. They were extremely nervous and watched with suspicion every move made by the staff, and this even though the men kept at the far end of the camp. I placed the meat next to my sleeping-hut at the opposite end, and within a few feet of the tree-bridge so that the family could quickly retreat unseen in case a visitor arrived. The cubs were thin but not unduly hungry so I assumed that Pippa must have killed at least once during the last five days. While I deticked and caressed her, she purred affectionately and licked my hand. This seemed to put the cubs at their ease and they soon started to eat. Unfortunately we did not have enough meat to give them a good meal, and what we had was rather high, so after a short while Pippa took the cubs across the tree bridge to the Gambo plain from where they all returned at sunset.

Meanwhile we had collected a fresh goat from Kenmare, on to whose carcass they now pounced greedily. While they fed I sat close to the family, guarding them against possible predators. Everything was still around us, except for the rhythmic humming of the crickets and cicadas which always started up their synchronized chorus after dark, and the munching of the cheetah. Undoubtedly the cheetah could hear a far greater variety of sounds than we could, and they kept on listening into the night, very tensely, until it was well after 8 p.m. when they went off across the rivulet. A little later, two lions roared not far away.

Under the circumstances, Pippa evidently regarded the camp as the safest place for she reappeared next afternoon. Soon after they had started eating John Baxendale drove up. Quickly, I sent Mary to stop him coming near, but the cubs had already bolted over the tree-bridge and only ventured back when Pippa called prr prr.

For two more days the family came into the camp, the cubs scared and jumpy as I had never before seen them, and I was not surprised when Pippa took them back to the Mulika plain. Since the last rains the grass there had grown dangerously high for cheetah, so Pippa spent a great deal of her time on trees watching out for prey or danger. Once she shared the same branch with a large hawk, who, waiting for meat scraps, remained most of the morning in position, ignoring our movements right beneath him – he was totally ignored by Pippa.

One day only the cubs came for the meat, while Pippa rested some 300 yards away. I took some food to her and patted her, but nothing would make her eat or drink. Instead she watched the plain most carefully and finally walked off sniffing the air. I sent Local to investigate but he found nothing which might have given cause to alarm her. As soon as the cubs realized that they were left alone, they got very upset. Big Boy seemed especially distressed and I heard him for the first time uttering the same low moan which Pippa always gave when she felt worried about the cubs. While he and Tiny nosed their way in the direction in which Pippa had disappeared, Somba grabbed all the meat she could hold between her teeth and only then trotted after them.

The cubs were growing fast and we had a tough time getting enough goats to satisfy their increasing appetites. Up to now, a boy had been in charge of the small herd at Kenmare Lodge, where he lived together with the two caretakers and their families. But the Lodge had gradually become so derelict that it was now decided to abandon the building and withdraw the caretakers. As it would have been unfair to let the youngster stay on alone, I had recently engaged an older man who was experienced in defending stock with his spear. When he and his wife arrived, I instructed him that, in the case of a predator attacking the goats, he was to report to me immediately and if possible provide us with evidence in the form of tracks of the predator or kill remains. All had gone well for a few days until the herdsman reported one morning that a lion had taken a goat the evening before but, as it had rained during the night, he could not trace the spoor this morning to bring back the remains of his kill.

Three days later he reported that two lions had taken two goats as soon as he had let them out in the morning. All the goats had scattered in the grass and he could not trace them, fearing the lions might be still close. I drove to George, who came over and searched the area thoroughly until it got dark, but he could not find the spoors of either stampeding goats or of any lion.

We badly needed meat for the cheetah, so next morning I drove to Kenmare to collect a fresh goat. I found the goats still locked up inside their hut, which had not been cleared for many days, and the herdsman still fast asleep. Drowsily he got up to clean the filth, while I followed his wife to one of the empty huts nearby. Inside I saw three goatskins pegged on to the ground, a cooking pot filled up with boiled meat, and half a goat carcass hung up for further meals. No wonder George did not find the remains of a kill let alone a lion spoor! I could sympathize with the man's anger when he found himself suddenly sacked and deprived of a life of leisure for which he was well paid, and one in which he was in sole command of a derelict lodge and every second day got a free goat by blaming its disappearance on an imaginary lion. Until I could find a more reliable herdsman, Stanley had to look after the goats, which meant that since Mary had also gone off for a week to Nairobi to settle some domestic problems which had developed since she had arrived in Kenya, Local and myself were left alone to care for the cheetah.

We plodded after them: I, laden with cameras, field-glasses, a tape-recorder and a megaphone; Local with the meat basket, water-can and rifle, until we found them far on the Mulika plain. During the following days they moved in

a large circle back to camp. This was the last place I wanted
the cubs to get used to, but all the tricks I invented to entice
the family away only resulted in their moving across the
rivulet, where they settled for the next days around the 'Kill
Acacia'.

One afternoon we found Pippa stalking a herd of twelve
waterbuck. She almost got a fawn but at the last moment was
thwarted by its mother. I was very worried watching the
antelope kicking at Pippa in defence of the fawn, since adult
waterbuck weigh up to 400 pounds, compared with Pippa's
weight which was at the most 120 pounds, and are therefore
formidable opponents.

Having failed to make a kill, Pippa turned up next morning
in camp with Somba and Tiny. There was no sign of Big Boy.
While I fed them, Local went to look for him and located him
far beyond the 'Kill Acacia'. He tried his best to make Big
Boy follow him, but had to return alone. We then cajoled the
rest of the family with meat into returning to the 'Kill Acacia'
to be within view of Big Boy. Although he must have seen us
carrying the meat basket, he did not budge, and only after we
had walked up to him did he join us back at the 'Kill Acacia'.
I could not understand his independent attitude as he was
only eight and a half months old, far too young to part from
Pippa, especially when he was hungry. And hungry he was,
judging by the way he now tucked into the meat.

Somba had been very friendly while eating earlier in camp,
but now she reverted to her aggressive food-defence tactics
and made such fierce attacks that I did not dare to move
during the time the family fed. When at last even Somba
could not hold any more meat, she followed the others to a
thornbush not far away where they had gone to sleep off their
full bellies. On her way, she passed Local and Stanley who had
been sitting quietly in the grass. I signalled the men to remain
absolutely still while Somba circled them and sniffed boldly at
their heads. It was a tricky situation, since the slightest wrong

movement from the men might have resulted in an injury, but both looked straight into Somba's eyes and betrayed no fear however close she came. At last she seemed satisfied and moved on to settle for a snooze.

Late in the afternoon the family again appeared in camp. I offered the cubs a little milk and Somba behaved quite differently despite my taking the bowl away from her while she was drinking to let the others have their share. By next morning the cheetah family had moved three miles from camp along the road to Leopard Rock. As soon as I bent low to hang the meat basket on a tree, Somba struck viciously at my head; it was fortunate that I was wearing my pith-helmet, if not she might have scalped me. She then controlled every movement of ours for a long time so that we could not feed the cheetah without being attacked by her. Finally she put her head into the milk bowl, which gave us a chance to get quickly at the meat. After she realized that nobody was going to deprive her of her ration, she settled down. At times Somba could be a real little shocker, but she was also endearing in her efforts to resolve her conflicting reactions; she would unfailingly charge anybody who dared to move while she was feeding on 'her ground', but when she ate in camp she never made defensive gestures. Since she so obviously differentiated between eating in the bush and in camp, I wondered if she felt that within a human settlement she was not in her own territory. Whatever her reasons, I was determined to keep the family away from the camp and to prevent the cubs from getting used to people more than was absolutely inevitable.

Recently I had often recorded the various cheetah sounds, most of which were strikingly similar to bird calls. Their high-pitched metallic chirps in particular were like those of a bird. Frequently I was misled by the birds during my searches, believing their chirps to be made by the cubs. I repeatedly played back my recordings to the cheetah, and they hardly took any notice of their own squeals while at loggerheads with each other, or their chirps, or purrs; but today, when I played back their fierce growls which I had taped the day before they all bolted instantly. We had had similar reactions from Elsa and her cubs who had ignored the playback of their own sounds but when they recognized the growls of the 'Fierce Lioness', their deadly enemy, they quickly ran off.

At this time George was looking after a little female lion cub, whose twin brother had been taken by a leopard. The mother was one of the lionesses which George had rehabilitated and though she had been a perfect mother, after the tragedy she had completely lost interest in the surviving cub. George had found her wandering hungry and alone, and she would certainly have died had he not adopted her. He named the cub Sandie and kept her confined within his camp. Sandie was a shy and wild little creature and rebuffed all our attempts to make friends with her. She would dash from one hiding-place to another when approached, growling and spitting whenever George offered her food. As often as I could spare the time, I helped to feed her. While crawling under beds and cars, playing hide-and-seek with her between petrol drums, or creeping through the maize patch which George's cook had planted near the kitchen shelter, I held out bowls of milk and small pieces of meat to her. Gradually I gained her trust, even to the extent of being able to pull the odd tick off her body, although I had to be careful not to overdo such familiarities. The only times when Sandie was happy and at her ease were when she heard a lion roaring far away, or when one of George's lions visited the camp. Then she would race up and down inside the wire, calling and calling, putting her small paw through the meshes in an attempt to touch her kin. But it would have been much too risky to allow her to join the pride before she was old enough to keep up with the movements of the adults. Although the mother had shown scant interest in Sandie when she saw her through the wire, she had given no signs of hostility. Therefore, some weeks later, George decided to let Sandie out in the presence of her mother, hoping for a reunion. As soon as the door was open, Sandie rushed joyfully to her mother, but instead of affection she received a savage bite. Poor little cub, she crept away and hid herself in the long grass outside the camp, where George had difficulty in finding her and bringing her back into the enclosure. Now she had to recover not only from her wound but also from the shock of being rejected by her mother. It was heartbreaking to see her watching her mother through the wire, sitting resigned and quiet and giving no displays of joy as she used to do. But this did not mean that Sandie was reconciled to captivity. Soon two of the younger lionesses belonging to George's pride seemed to be taking a growing interest in her, and it was wonderful to observe how the bond between them developed, even though they were separated by the wire. Finally, Sandie took the law into her own paws and escaped to freedom and her friends.

Sandie's determination not to become tame, as well as the reaction of Pippa's cubs to my camp, convinced me that one could help both lion and cheetah from becoming exterminated by bringing cubs up from the earliest age under natural conditions until they were mature and able themselves to breed wild cubs.

Meanwhile, one morning Somba behaved more wildly than I appreciated, splashing the whole bowl of milk into my face. She was so savage that I wondered if she were a freak. But even if this were so, it would be most interesting to see how Pippa would cope with her. Up to now she had handled her amazingly well.

The general belief that cheetah are timid and harmless compared with lion and leopard is only justified in that they are not man-eaters; otherwise, they can be very dangerous when provoked. I once witnessed such an incident when I was visiting the Olduway Gorge near the Serengeti. Driving out of the gorge, we saw an old Masai supporting a boy who, covered in blood, could hardly move. From what we could make out of the old man's excited chatter the story was a gruesome one. The youngster had been herding stock when he saw a cheetah stalking one of the goats. Trying to defend his charges, he hurled his spear at the cheetah, but missed, and found himself without a weapon when the cheetah turned on him. He then attacked the animal with his knife and got severely mauled while stabbing it. Finally the knife got stuck in the cheetah's body and it ran off, leaving a trail of blood behind it. Hearing the yells of the youth, the old Masai came rushing to his help and saw the cheetah disappearing into a thicket far away. We took the injured boy to the headquarters of Olduway camp where his wounds were disinfected and dressed before he was taken to a hospital. I was of course interested to know what had happened to the cheetah, and drove back to the scene. There we found several Masai already circling the thicket with their spears and throwing stones into it to chase the cheetah out. When they asked me for a match to set the bush alight, I explained that I was a non-smoker and therefore carried no matches. Undeterred they reverted to the ancient method of making fire by twiddling a stick against a wooden block until the friction causes the wood to smoulder and it blows into a flame. While they concentrated on doing this, I searched around the thicket and was relieved to find no trace of a cheetah's spoor anywhere near.

Lately Pippa had behaved rather aloofly, and reduced our time together strictly to her feeding hours. Before Mary's arrival she had always shown her affection by brushing herself suddenly against me, spanking my legs, nibbling my hand in a playful way, purring and looking with soft eyes at me when she was happy. In short, we both knew that we were pals. Now there were many people around and we were never left alone for such intimacies; whatever Pippa did, she either got a microphone held close to her face, cameras focused on her, or cars passing with strange people watching her through binoculars.

Like Elsa, Pippa hated to be photographed, and worse still, to be sketched. Both animals seemed to be acutely aware whether they were being treated subjectively or objectively;

they knew when I looked at them for their own sake, or if I was merely using them as a model, and this even though my outward behaviour was just the same.

Now I was painfully conscious that our intimate relationship had been injured. Of course, I had only brought Mary daily together with the family as I wanted them to make friends with her specifically because I knew that I would soon have to go to London for another operation on my hand, and hoped that by then she would have won the trust of the cheetah and be able to look after them in my absence. Explaining my recent estrangement from Pippa to Mary, we agreed that from now on she would only stay with the family during the feeding time and afterwards sit in the car and read while I would follow them and remain with Pippa for as long as it might take to restore our old relationship. It was touching to see how quickly Pippa reacted the next day to our being alone together. As soon as all the family had had their fill, they moved out of view of Mary and the men. I followed them and stretched myself between Pippa and her cubs who cuddled up into a soft heap under a shady bush. After I had caressed Pippa for a while, she put her head close to mine and purred so strongly that I felt her body shaking with the vibrations. I knew that I was again accepted into her world, and was determined to guard our privacy from now on as carefully as I could. Pippa seemed to feel the same because it became almost a ritual for her to share a time alone with me every day and she was most cunning at securing this privilege.

The family had lately remained within a mile of the 'Photo Tree', where Pippa had got into the habit of resting on the roof of the Land-Rover to escape the boisterous games of the cubs. They never followed her up to her lofty retreat, but after they had exhausted themselves in chasing each other around and wanted to go off to rest, they called in sharp, metallic chirps for their mother to come down. Somba had by far the loudest call and it needed no words to interpret their impatience when Pippa ignored her children's chirping chorus.

One morning the cubs were most intrigued by something in the grass. Judging by their cautious movements and frequent regressions, I assumed it to be a snake. Grabbing a stick, I then (with equal caution) walked closer until I recognized a monitor. This large but harmless lizard had had its retreat cut off and all it could do to keep the cubs at bay was to blow itself up threateningly, like a dragon, while thrashing its tail and hissing so alarmingly that even I got scared in spite of knowing that it was only bluff. However it seemed that my appearance, in addition to that of the cubs, was more than the monitor could bear, and so with unbelievable courage and speed it wriggled off, hissing as it ran between the perplexed cubs. They did not pursue it, but walked slowly away as if nothing had happened.

Later on they rejoined Pippa at the 'Photo Tree'. Somba was more friendly than I had ever seen her before, despite the fact that her gums, as well as those of Big Boy, were bleeding between the lower canines and premolars. Tiny seemed off-colour and behaved in a restrained manner. Whenever Pippa gently clouted him, as if to encourage him to take part in the games, he walked quietly away and watched the others with his large, sensitive eyes from a safe distance. How like he was to Mbili when she was his age, and how similar was my anxiety for both. Maybe the cubs had teething trouble? They were now nine months old and, compared to Pippa's previous litter when they had reached that age, permanent teeth should now be through. A few days later, Local spotted the family near the Hans Lugga close to where Mbili had submitted to Pippa five months before. She had now definitely taken possession of her daughter's territory. As her own ground was no longer swampy there seemed to be no excuse for a temporary occupation of Mbili's area. Not long after this Local saw Mbili within 400 yards of the 'Photo Tree' which was also in her domain. She let him come close enough to identify her clearly but ran away whenever he came too near. So as not to frighten her away, he left Mbili and came to collect me, but when we returned, she was gone. From her spoor we learned that she had crossed the road before Pippa and her cubs had walked along it to their daily playground at the 'Photo Tree' where we found them waiting for us. Poor Mbili, she had obviously given way to Pippa, who had now resided in her territory for several weeks.

Mbili, Whity and Tatu were two years and eight months old, and it was fourteen and a half months since I had fed all three together for the last time. Whenever we had seen them since, they had been in excellent condition and all were larger than their mother.

One evening I found a young mousebird in my sleeping-hut. Not yet able to fly, it flapped and hopped clumsily about until I noticed that it used only one leg – the other leg being a mere stump. Quickly, I lined a cardboard box with grass, placed the terrified bird inside, and during the night kept it close to me. Before dawn it started to cry. I tried in vain to feed it bread crumbs and birdseed, until I heard the call of its mother coming from a nearby thicket. I then put 'Stumpy' as close as I could to her, the fledgling fluttered unsteadily and scrambled up into the thorny labyrinth, but soon it lost its balance and hung by its one leg, dangling helplessly upside down. When I rescued Stumpy, I was amazed at how calmly it accepted my help. But by the time I had put it down on the grass the mother had flown away and, though I waited for some time for her return, she seemed to have abandoned the chick. I now tried my luck with feeding banana to the hungry little bird; this it liked and took greedily from my hand. In the evening, while keeping it again inside the box near my bed, I watched it pecking vigorously at more banana and so was glad to see that at least Stumpy would not starve. Next morning it ventured straight to the thicket from where its mother was calling. Now, for the next few days, she took over the feeding while I was allowed to rescue Stumpy whenever I found him dangling head down from a twig. Sharing the care of the little bird with its mother during the day, and keeping it protected for the next three nights, I watched it one morning fly high up into a tamarind tree, where it perched well on one leg. When later in the day I saw it and its mother flying off, I felt extremely happy to know that Stumpy was now strong enough to master life, even with only one leg.

Less satisfactory was my experience with the tiny, pinhead-sized bugs which at that time suddenly invaded my camp. They neither stung nor bit, but – covering the vegetation along the rivulets in thick layers – they ate every green blade and leaf until even the magnificent tamarinds were reduced to wooden skeletons. Walking under the trees was like being in a snow-storm; the bugs dropped on to our hair, into the eyes, on to the typewriter and the camera, excreting a most unpleasant smell as soon as we squashed them. Having been used to living all day in the open, we now became almost prisoners inside the palm-log huts, except for the early morning and late afternoon when these stinkers were less active. Invasions by these bugs are rare in Kenya, but I had been warned that when one took place it would last up to three months or more unless the insects were sprayed with insecticide. However, as I did not want to poison the birds and other harmless insects as well, I put up with the unpleasant bugs, hoping that the next rains would drown the lot.

Mary's domestic troubles now reached a crisis and she decided to return to the USA – we parted within a few days. This left me in an awkward position as I was due to go to London shortly.

Until I found another assistant, I made the best of being alone with the cheetah, again I spent a whole day with them.* The cubs were nine and a half months old and still their gums were bleeding; I concluded from this that their permanent teeth were not yet fully developed. This might explain why Pippa did not allow them to join her in stalking a herd of

* See Appendix II.

Grant. However much they trembled with excitement, they remained rigid until Tiny finally broke away and spoiled the hunt.

During the midday rest the cubs, except Tiny, took turns with Pippa in looking out for danger. Tiny did not even raise his head as he snuggled up to Big Boy and looked around with his large soft eyes wonderingly, trusting that all was safe. He seemed more interested in catching Somba's tail whenever she passed close to him on her patrols, watching with hard, contracted pupils and tight lips every moving thing in the area. Pippa was, of course, the most alert of all.

Later, Somba gave a perfect demonstration of 'marking territory' by defecating in a very uncomfortable position on a fallen tree exactly at the spot where she had done this twice before.

A few days later, Pippa again brought the cubs into camp. They had been missing for forty-eight hours and were hungry. Luckily I had sent for a goat that morning. I now asked two men to kill it inside their hut before Pippa could get hold of it. I did not know that the hut was already crowded with Local's wife, her sister and Local's youngest child, all of whom he had kept hidden there since early morning. So when the goat was pushed inside the hut, in the nick of time, it was greeted with protesting screams from the women, to which the goat responded with loud bleatings. Attracted by the noise, the cubs raced frantically round the hut, while Pippa tried to jump on to the roof but only succeeded in tearing off part of its palm-leaf thatching. As a result of all this, the bedlam inside became ear-splitting and was increased by Local yelling comforting shouts from the outside to his terrified family. I could not help laughing for Local knew that it was strictly against the rules for him to bring his family here, and nothing could have taught him a better lesson than the present brawl. Later, after giving him hell for bringing his harem along, I asked him to take them away immediately. Finally we managed to divert the cheetah's interest and the goat carcass was

'Acrobatics'

They often retired to a tree

At loggerheads on the tree bridge

Joy feeding one of the cubs, 5 months old

Somba 'marking territory'

Somba

opposite
Somba could not believe it – her bone had dropped
into the water

The cubs before a storm breaks

On a termite hill

Last photo of Pippa with her cubs

The cubs on their own, 44 days after Pippa's death

Pippa in the Animal Orphanage

safely taken to a place where they could eat it in peace.

As soon as all had had their fill, they crossed over the tree-bridge, Somba, as usual, carrying a bone. As she tried to get a better grip on it, the bone fell into the water. Dumfounded, she watched it disappear, then ran down the bank and performed most daring acrobatics at the flooded rivulet trying to recover the precious object. Twice she returned to the bridge, cocking her head to find a new angle; finally she gave up.

The rains had started a few days earlier and the sky looked threateningly black all round. That night it poured non-stop from 9 p.m. till dawn. By then the tree-bridge was half under water. As soon as it was light, I saw the cheetah crossing it very cautiously to get the remains of the goat. I expected them to keep on our side of the flooded rivulet so as not to get cut off from their food supply, but as soon as they had eaten, Pippa took the cubs back across the bridge and on to the Gambo plain. By lunchtime the water had receded to normal, and the road was dry enough for motoring again.

A little later John Baxendale drove into camp with my new assistant. We had met some time ago when he had visited the Park with his parents. They had recently inquired if I could help young Ben to spend some time in the bush as he wanted to study birds. Since he could combine this with the work I needed done, I offered him the job. He could start at once as he was a Kenya citizen and therefore needed no work permit. John had collected the lad from a farm a few hundred miles away.

While we were chatting, the cheetah reappeared in camp. Pippa inspected the newcomer carefully. Finally she allowed him to stroke her. As a last test, she nibbled at his hand, and when she had thus assured herself that Ben was 'safe', she called prr prr to the cubs. I was very glad about this friendly reception since we had only a week left for Ben and the cheetah to get to know each other. They played quite at ease around us for an hour, after which Pippa led the cubs across the tree-bridge. When she had reached the middle of the narrow trunk, she sat down, blocking the way. The cubs nudged and prodded her, but Pippa would not budge. Since the trunk was only wide enough for one animal to walk along it at a time, it needed careful trapeze tricks on the part of the cubs to clamber one after the other across their mother without slipping and falling into the water below. Only after all had safely scrambled over her did she leave her precarious position and follow the family to the far bank. I could not make out why she had insisted on being an obstacle to the cubs on such a narrow bridge – perhaps she wanted to teach them to have complete control over their movements.

Next morning, Local found the family at the 'Kill Acacia'. They followed him to the camp, but as I did not want them to get used to human habitations, we enticed them with meat back to the Gambo plain where we fed them. All seemed to accept Ben, except for Somba who crouched low and did her striking act whenever he became too familiar.

To make the most of the few days we had left together, we visited the family again at teatime. They had not moved far. Afterwards we strolled together for about a mile, until we spotted a few Grevy's zebra intermingled with a herd of waterbuck, and two small fawns. As soon as Pippa started to stalk them, we withdrew and made a long detour in order not to interfere with the hunt. Struggling through thorny bush, we arrived in camp after dark – only to find the cheetah waiting for us! What fools we felt. I gave the cubs milk – hoping that Pippa would take the hint and go off and kill. Soon after this, they vanished into the night. If I was determined to force Pippa to hunt she was equally determined to get food in camp, and she turned up at dawn the following day. Again we carried the meat across the rivulet on to the Gambo plain, where we left the family to feed. But our triumph was short-lived, as in the early afternoon they reappeared in camp. Now it became a game between Pippa and me to see who was the more determined, and off we went together once more to try Pippa's luck with the zebra and waterbuck who were still where we had met them the day before. For some strange reason, the cubs remained about 600 yards behind while Pippa stalked the fawns and got very close to one. She was still stalking when it became too dark for us to watch.

Evidently she failed to catch it, as the whole family turned up in camp next morning, very hungry. I was exasperated. How could I break this new habit of using the camp as a feeding-place, when for almost ten months Pippa had avoided it. Perseveringly, we again carried the meat on to the Gambo plain, but Pippa remained resolutely in camp. There were now only four days before I had to leave for London and so, to remain in their good books, I weakened, and fed them all in camp. Pippa had won the game.

Soon after this, they moved along the road for half a mile to a murram mound, which provided an ideal look-out and playground in the cooler hours of the day. While the cubs had glorious games sliding down the loose gravel, Pippa dozed some 300 yards away. At teatime, we returned and found the cheetah where we had left them in the morning, all resting on top of the mound which was partly overgrown with pentanisia. Silhouetted against an intensely blue sky and surrounded by the sky-blue flowers, the golden cheetah looked superb. I could not resist joining them, and while I caressed Pippa the cubs fondled each other as well as their mother, accepting me quite naturally as part of their family. Later I took a lot of photographs, and sketched Pippa with a sad heart, fearing that these might be the last pictures I would be able to make of my friends for a long time to come. I lingered on until it got dark and we had to return. Near camp, I suddenly felt Pippa brushing against my knee – she had followed us, alone. We waited some time for the cubs, then returned to the murram mound to look for them, but there was no response to any of my calls. Pippa walked around undecidedly, in silence, then she disappeared into the dark. Although we were only half a mile from camp, it was strange that she should have deserted the cubs after dark at that early age. There was nothing we could do until next morning, when at daybreak we continued our search.

We found the family a mile upstream, all very hungry. It was drizzling, and Somba seemed puzzled by my new raincoat, and promptly charged. After I had taken it off, she settled to her meal and was at loggerheads with Pippa for a long time, holding her head down while growling fiercely. Pippa, of course, could have easily put Somba in her place, but I assumed that this was the way in which she educated the cubs to defend their food.

For the next few days, Pippa brought the cubs into camp, however hard I tried to feed them away from it. Even on our last morning together – the 10th of May – they all turned up at dawn and we had quite a job carrying a goat carcass across the rivulet with all the cheetah dancing around us until we reached the 'Kill Acacia' where we fed them. There was nothing unusual in this scene, except for my feelings. I knew that I had to be away for at least three months and naturally was distressed. I hesitated to interpret Pippa's recent frequent visits to the camp as a response to the anxiety I felt in view of my forthcoming departure, or to believe that she might wish to be as close to me during this time as I indeed wanted to be to her. There had in fact been previous incidents of our mutual 'sharing' for which I could find no explanation except by believing that Pippa 'knew'. Now I could only pray that all would go well during my absence.

After the family had completed their meal, I followed them to a small patch of forest into the shade of which they all disappeared, except Somba who had loitered behind to finish off the last scraps of meat and now seemed to be lost. Clambering up a small tree, she called in piercing chirps which I recorded on the tape. She then hopped off and ran away to join the others . . . However painful it was for me to tear myself away, I knew at least that Ben would do his best to look after my friends who had already taken to him surprisingly well. I had arranged that he should write me detailed reports twice a week. I left him enough money to buy ample provisions for himself and to secure a steady supply of goats; I also gave him the addresses of two vets in case one was unavailable; and I left him my Land-Rover and Local and Stanley to help with the cheetah; and the cook to do all the work in the camp. Then, hoping for the best, I set off for London.

8. The Cheetah in Foster Care

I had been booked for a major operation for transplanting tendons from my leg to my hand and it was due to take place immediately on my arrival. But when the surgeon examined my hand, he insisted not only on physiotherapy treatment for several weeks before the operation could take place, but also on more treatment of the same kind afterwards. This would mean an absence from the cheetah of five months. I was most depressed.

During the trying period I spent in London, I only ever felt relaxed when letters from Ben assured me that all was well.

According to him, Pippa had stopped her visits to the camp immediately after my departure and moved upstream to the Gambo plain. There he found the cubs on the 12th of May, but they took no notice of his calls. However, after a while, Somba came along and reacted in a very friendly way when he offered her milk. Meanwhile Big Boy and Tiny walked off some hundred yards to join Pippa. When Somba and the men followed, they found them on a freshly-killed female Grant. Somba instantly changed her attitude and behaved very aggressively towards Ben. Pippa had only just started eating; she and Big Boy were on the front quarters, and the other cubs at the back under the tail. It took them one and a half hours to finish the young gazelle, leaving the leg bones and part of the head.

A few days later, while searching for the family, Ben heard Pippa calling the cubs who soon came rushing towards her. When he approached, she stopped the cubs and went up to examine him thoroughly. He was wearing a new shirt. Only after she had made sure who he was did she call the cubs. I had previously observed similar incidents with Pippa and her second litter, as well as with Elsa and her cubs. There are authentic records of two keepers who were actually killed by lions and tigers when entering their cages in strange garments. I am puzzled that these cats should not rely more on permanent characteristics such as scent, likeness and movements when identifying their human friends, and I wonder if the reason why they react so suspiciously to unfamiliar clothing may be in fact that animals do not change their skin as we do our clothes.

During the next weeks, Pippa widened her territory. He thought it significant that she staked out a different terrain from the one she had selected as the hunting-ground for her previous litter. This was in line with her decision to avoid taking the present cubs to the same trees or termite hills that Whity, Mbili and Tatu had used as their playgrounds (with the exception of the 'Kill Acacia').

She now concentrated on the area around the Rojoweru and four of its tributaries, which watered the hilly plains beyond the new headquarters. She also made good use of the new airstrip there, as she had previously done with the airstrip at Leopard Rock when she had the other cubs. Ben wrote that the family was often to be seen there in the early mornings chasing ostrich, Grant, or guinea fowl. Once, when Pippa was concentrating on a wart-hog, Tiny pretended to stalk it, while uttering strange new sounds like a person humming.

Of course all wild animals use the airstrips in every National Park, either for hunting or as a playground, but I was concerned in case Pippa's family might get used to human activities, such as the maintenance of airstrips, and I therefore wrote to Ben that he should try to entice the cheetah away from it.

A few days later, he located them five miles off at the Hans Lugga, where they had obviously just killed, for their bellies were bulging and Big Boy still had blood around his mouth. Ben offered the cubs milk, after which Somba came up to him and, licking his knees, sat down beside him and even placed her paw in his hand. A few minutes later, she and Pippa went off, with Big Boy and Tiny following at a distance. It was in this order that the family now often moved around.

One day Somba was bitten by ants; she must have believed that the meat she had been eating was infested by them for she spat at it, and then hit out at it with her paws, but when after a short while she discovered her mistake she continued eating.

On one occasion the cheetah were playing on the airstrip when a wart-hog came quite close. Big Boy promptly chased after it until he got within twenty yards, then he stopped. The wart-hog turned round to face him, Big Boy instantly sat down and watched the wart-hog trot away. I well remember a similar incident between Pippa's previous litter and a wart-hog when they were at the same age – about eleven months.

After six weeks, the family turned up in camp and stayed two days. The following morning, Ben went early to Kenmare to collect a goat, while Local searched for the cheetah in the vicinity of the Lodge. Suddenly he was charged by Somba, who came rushing out from thick bush. Later Ben found the rest of the family some hundred yards away on a kill. They had eaten most of it, with the exception of the hind legs and the head, from which he could identify a young male water-buck with horns only a few inches long. Ben later added this to the collection of trophies and lower jaws which I had started making of all the kills the cheetah made. He was charged by Somba when he came within twenty yards of the kill. As usual, he gave the cubs milk and, after drinking, Somba settled down but rested right on the head of the kill to make sure that nobody could interfere with it. The men then walked back to camp for their breakfast. On their return they saw hundreds of vultures heading in the same direction and then swooping down to the kill. There, they found Somba gallantly guarding the bare bones from the descending birds, but on seeing the men appear, she let them take over the defence and joined the rest of the family who were sleeping off their full bellies.

That night two lionesses passed by the camp, with the result that the cheetah cleared out. Five nights later, Boy and Suswa (another of the lions George was looking after) walked right through my camp and crossed the bridge below the kitchen.

In the morning, the men located Pippa's family some eight miles distant at the Rojoweru where they had killed another waterbuck, this time a female, slightly smaller than the last kill. Somba duly defended it and charged the intruders, but later allowed Ben to photograph the remains of the carcass from a distance of ten feet. When the men returned a few hours later, hoping to rescue some of the meat, Somba would not let anyone get near, even though there was nothing left to defend. This was the fourth kill in the one and a half months since I had left Meru.

Up to now (the end of June) all had gone very well and I felt most grateful to young Ben; my only complaint was about his habit of handling all the cheetah frequently. I had always taken the utmost care not to get the cubs used to the human touch, so that they would find it easier to forget our relationship once they were ready to live independently. I was also surprised to learn that Ben's parents had been camping within a hundred and fifty yards of my camp during their visit to Meru, and I had to ask him to choose a camp-site for them farther away. The Park Warden had recently asked Ben to collect birds for the Park. He had in fact refrained from shooting them within a hundred yards of the camp, but I now asked him to extend this safety belt to at least five times the distance. It had taken me a long time to win the trust of all the animals around the camp, to let them know they were safe in our presence. I found it most enjoyable and also of immense interest to watch their natural behaviour intimately, as I was able to do once they had accepted us as harmless and even protective. Every morning I had fed the birds before I had

my breakfast; first the tiny red-billed firefinches and 'cordon
bleu' descended from the nearby bushes to the millet – they
had to be quick to get their share before the black-headed
weavers interfered, adding their golden plumage to the already
colourful crowd. They in their turn were driven off by the
belligerent ring-necked doves, who pecked at the smaller birds,
until they all gave way to the one grey-headed bush shrike
who held the floor whenever he appeared. He was a very
handsome bird with his green back and yellow underpart, but
was obviously not popular. While this little war went on outside, some fifteen 'Superb Starlings' often invaded my dining-
hut where I had breakfast, to wait for the fatty bacon rind and
cheese crumbs which I could not cut up quickly enough. One
of these truly superbly-coloured starlings became almost a pet
and would fearlessly hop on to my foot if I dared to ignore his
screams for more than was his share of the meal, with the result
that on many occasions the starlings had my breakfast, while
I had to be content with fruit and an egg.

These birds were almost tame by now, as were the wiretails
who had nested for six generations inside the studio-hut. I
loved my feathery friends who woke me up each morning with
a sleepy twitter which gradually crescendoed into a jubilant
chorus to welcome the new day and I was truly alarmed to
think that all their trust might now be broken, and only hoped
that no damage had already been done.

It always intrigued me how Pippa managed not to clash
with the lions who so frequently shared her hunting-grounds.
Now I heard that Ugas had recently spent the night in our
camp – and that the airstrip at headquarters was occupied by
a lioness. Pippa must have watched her from a safe distance
because she immediately reclaimed this favourite playground
once the lioness had moved on. There Ben found the family,
bulging with meat. It was less than a week since Pippa had
last killed. Although the men could find no trace of the carcass,
they assumed it to have been a wart-hog as the next day they
saw only three on the runway instead of the usual family of

our. They now manœuvred these three towards the cheetah
until they came face to face within thirty yards of each other.
Suddenly the wart-hogs stopped, undecided what to do on
finding themselves cornered between the men and the cheetah.
They decided in favour of the cheetah, and were promptly
chased by Tiny and Somba, who, however, soon gave up, but
Tiny persevered and almost caught a pig. Pippa had been
watching this game, and when Tiny returned to her she not
only ambushed him but knocked him over.

He was growing very quickly and was now nearly as large
as Big Boy. He guarded his food most efficiently and stood his
ground so well in all their skirmishes that it was Somba who
was in need of protection from her boisterous brothers. While
the family played round the Land-Rover, Somba discovered
the side mirror and, jumping up and down on the bonnet,
seemed puzzled by her image.

For five days Ben fed the family on the airstrip until they
disappeared again. He traced them across the Rojoweru River
which was deep at that spot and too wide to jump. On the
far bank dense bush covered a slope leading to plains, which
extended for several miles until they adjoined the large swamp
near George's camp. On these plains about a mile from where
the cheetah had crossed the river, the men found the remains
of an adult female Grant surrounded by the fresh spoor of
cheetah – but of the family they saw no sign.

For a week they screened this new area thoroughly, frequently finding spoor but never getting a glimpse of the
animals. Finally, the family re-crossed the Rojoweru and returned to their old hunting-grounds – and all met again about
three miles from the headquarters. The cheetah were hungry
but otherwise so fit that Pippa must have killed at least once
more during the last week.

The cubs were now exactly one year old and – judging by
the frequency of the kills – assisted Pippa in the hunts. Ever
since I had left Meru three months ago, the cubs had often
rested a little way off from Pippa. This distance now increased

to a quarter of a mile, and often the family were united only
during mealtimes. The men were therefore not surprised at
seeing Pippa alone next morning, but were puzzled as to why
she did not help them to find the cubs. During the half-hour
in which they searched every bush and called, she showed no
concern but dozed under a tree; and when at last the men
located the cubs over 400 yards from her, they seemed quite
indifferent to Pippa's presence, although they soon joined together for feeding.

I was amused to read how Tiny stole the meat from his big
brother, and got away with it. I could hardly believe that Tiny
was no longer the timid, gentle runt, but now challenged
everybody fearlessly, just for the fun of it. I was also surprised to learn that he and Big Boy had recently become
aware of the attraction of the female of the species and took
turns to flirt with Somba. She seemed to enjoy their affectionate lickings and playful teasings until their antics got too
rough and she escaped to Pippa, who watched over the growing independence of her children.

She was obviously loosening her maternal ties, but when
there was the slightest sign of danger she never left the cubs.
So when next morning the men found leopard spoor mixed up
with the pugmarks of the family, and also identified Ugas'
pugmarks by his malformed toe, they knew that they were
again in for a long search. During the days following the
cheetah appeared and disappeared erratically; most of the
time the whereabouts of the family could only be traced by
their spoor. One day it led through a belt of bush on to vast
plains towards the Murera. This attractive river had recently
been made accessible to visitors by the Golo Circuit which
starting at Leopard Rock, followed along its palm-covered
banks for about ten miles, then crossed into arid scrub country
which was alive with gerenuk, rhino, buffalo, giraffe, eland
zebra, Grant, and more dik-dik than anywhere else inside the
Park, until it reached the Rojoweru and continued along it for
some miles to Kenmare. Including the road which connected

the Lodge with Leopard Rock and passed by my camp — the circle covered thirty-five miles. The cheetah had recently frequented the area because of the many smaller antelopes such as dik-dik, duiker and Grant that lived there.

While the men were tracking the spoor, they were not surprised to see vultures circling close to the Golo Circuit. Walking in their direction to investigate, a black-maned lion got up some hundred yards in front of them; unaware of the party behind him, he also followed the vultures until he came within fifty yards of the kill. Ben then saw Pippa and the cubs get up and dash off. He called out, and startled by his voice, the lion bolted. Pippa instantly chased him off for good. A few minutes later, the family reunited at the remains of a Grevy's zebra foal. It could not have been more than a month old; nevertheless, it was interesting that the cheetah had tackled the young of such big animals, risking the powerful kicks of the mother. There was nothing left of the carcass for the men to recover for the next day's meal, so they left the family to sleep off their bulging bellies.

In spite of this feast — which was the third kill that week — when the men located them the following morning the cheetah were again on the hunt. Pippa was high up in a tree and had spotted a herd of Grant. To get a better look, she climbed another tree and watched the gazelles for a long time. She then jumped to the ground, called the cubs, and with Somba at her side, Tiny fifty yards behind and Big Boy still farther back, they crept through the grass taking careful advantage of the smallest scrap of cover, until they were close. Unfortunately, Somba showed herself too soon and that was the end of the hunt. To compensate the hungry family, Ben fed them the meat he had brought along until Pippa retreated to a shady tree. The cubs played around a little and wanted to join her, but she moved off immediately to another lair. A short while later Somba and Tiny made another attempt to rest with her, but again Pippa left the minute the cubs sat down. Meanwhile, Big Boy, finding himself deserted, called.

His voice was still breaking and his throat sounded very sore. Tiny rushed hurriedly back to keep him company, while Somba succeeded in snuggling up to Pippa.

Two days later the family were luckier and killed a young waterbuck. I was relieved and proud that Pippa and her cubs now killed frequently, but was terrified when Ben wrote that a gang of poachers had recently been operating right inside the Park and had killed rhino, leopard and three cheetah. For some time we had lost track of Whity, Mbili and Tatu, and I was tormented by the fear that one of them might have fallen victim to the poachers. My method of identifying Pippa's cubs by the individual patterns of tail-root spots, could now be of the greatest value and I asked Ben to recover, if possible, the skins of the dead cheetah. Later I learned that the poachers had cut up the pelts before they were arrested.

The news about Pippa and her present litter continued to be excellent. The brothers seemed devoted to each other and almost inseparable; Tiny was by now the equal of Big Boy and spent a great part of his time climbing trees, at which he excelled Somba who only climbed occasionally, while Big Boy hardly ever joined in this game. Big Boy was already taller at the shoulder than Pippa, with Tiny not quite as large as she, and Somba the smallest of the lot.

The family moved on an average one to two miles a day and rarely slept at the same place twice. Although Pippa spent most of her resting time apart from the cubs, she never deserted them for a full day, at least as far as could be judged from their spoor.

On the 24th of August the men located the cubs close to the road, halfway between the camp and 'Mile 5'. A few minutes later, Pippa appeared, with a female kongoni following her slowly. The hartebeest was at times within five yards of Pippa who would then lie down, while the kongoni stopped. As soon as Pippa got up to advance towards the antelope it would move back a step or two. This strange procession continued until a young kongoni fawn suddenly emerged from the grass about thirty yards from Pippa, who instantly ran after it, and after about sixty paces brought it down by placing her paw on its back. She then grabbed its throat and held on to its windpipe. Meanwhile, the mother tried to defend her young, and for a moment it looked as though Pippa might have to let it go but Somba succeeded in driving the kongoni away. She chased her for some 300 yards, by which time the fawn was dead. When the mother returned and realized the tragedy she put up no resistance, and after Somba had chased her off a second time she did not come back. It had taken Pippa two minutes to suffocate the little fawn, helped by Big Boy and Tiny who started eating it before it was dead. In forty-five minutes there was nothing left, other than the head and leg bones.

It was the first time any of us had witnessed the actual killing of a prey, let alone the teamwork between Pippa and her cubs to make it a success. When Ben measured the distance over which the hunt had taken place, he learned that from her standing position Pippa had chased sixty paces to catch the escaping calf which had run thirty paces – thus she had covered twice the distance the calf had in the same time. This was the sixth kill made by the family within twenty-four days. During the next nine days, the family made four more kills; two young waterbuck and a gerenuk, the last kill only known by their full bellies and blood-covered faces.

Despite all this splendid news, I became increasingly depressed in England. The strain of living in London after having been used to unlimited space and an outdoor life was more than I could take, especially during the summer months. Luckily I had some very good friends in Surrey, with whom I later stayed, and their wonderful hospitality and beautiful gardens helped me through a most trying period. I travelled daily for an hour, on overcrowded trains, in to London, and then by the still more stuffy underground to Kensington where I had my physiotherapeutic treatment. Walking the last part through Hyde Park to my destination, I often hummed the little tune which I sang whenever I wanted the cheetah to follow me – 'Pippa Pippa Pippalunka and the little Cubserle, Come on, Come on, Come on, Come on, Come on . . .' and I imagined the sinewy, graceful animals moving beside me to the rhythm of this song and often when I was hanging on to anything firm in a full bus and bumping against my standing neighbours I day-dreamed of resting close to the family and feeling their bodies shaken by their contented purrs.

I was most interested in learning how the Whipsnade Zoo in Bedfordshire had succeeded in breeding cheetah, and as soon as I could I visited it. Here the animals are not caged. The Director kindly let me read the files on Juanita's history, who up to date had borne two litters of one male and two females.* From this I learned that of the first litter, born in 1967, two of the cubs soon died of osteodystrophic lesions and the surviving cub was still very ill. The second litter, born in July 1968, was now exactly one year old and thriving. I found these cubs huddled together in the centre of a comparatively small paddock which contained a bushy tree with branches but these were too thin to carry the weight of a cheetah. At the far end was a wooden shelter adjoining a small enclosure where the sick cheetah of the first litter rested. Except for their sleeping-hut there was no place for the cubs to hide in or climb up to. They had been moved from a large compound to this small place so that the visitors could see them all the time. Knowing how dependent Pippa's families were on exercise, privacy and concealment, I wondered if these cubs would ever breed.

The three cheetah at the Regent's Park Zoo in the centre of London were much worse off. Each had a tiny enclosure, with a wooden hut in one corner, and pebbled ground, which of course was easier to clean than grass but unnatural to a cheetah. They could rub noses through the wire, or face leopards, lions and tigers in their compounds across a narrow path, from which visitors could compare the various cat

* Manton Report – Appendix III.

species. Seeing the indifference of these cheetah to the lions and leopards, I realized again how much wild animals are bound to suffer in order to adapt their instincts to an artificial life in which they lose their fear of even their most dreaded enemies.

It was a rainy, cold afternoon, and one of the cheetah shivered more than a normal reaction to the bad weather would have warranted. When a new cloud-burst drenched it, the animal looked miserable but remained immobile instead of going inside its hut for shelter as his pals did. I called a keeper and asked if this cheetah were ill, but he said there was nothing wrong with the animal except that it would not use the hut because it disliked the smell of its recent occupant. Looking at the rain-loaded sky, I suggested that the hut should be changed, but was assured that nothing could be done until the next day when the Head Keeper would be there. I insisted that at least a temporary shelter be put in to give the sick animal protection from the rain, and waited until this was done.

How could a cheetah feel relaxed under such conditions, let alone mate and breed? I had a long talk with the Director, in which I stressed that exercise and privacy were far more important for cheetah than for other cats. I pointed out that Pippa's territory in the Meru Park was sixty-three square miles, in which she roamed freely with her cubs. Since no zoo could ever provide sufficient space to satisfy a cheetah, and since it was not their function to conceal the animals from visitors, it seemed a waste of time, risk and money to try to breed cheetah in captivity (which would in any case only produce more pets or zoo-exhibits) if one could breed these sensitive animals under natural conditions. Pippa had proved that this could be done, and up to now she had borne, in four litters, fifteen cubs, of which six were still alive. Since Pippa was barely five years old and the lifespan of cheetah is approximately fifteen years, she could be expected to triple the number of surviving cubs to eighteen, which would all go on breeding and thus restock the bush with wild-born cheetah. I further urged that because cheetah are second on the list of 'Endangered Animals' no time should be lost in building up a healthy survival number in the areas in which the animals could go on breeding.

I also visited the Norfolk Wildlife Park, where Philip Wayre was successfully breeding pheasants, European lynx and other animals. He is the Chairman of the Conservation and Breeding Committee of Great Britain and Ireland and so was interested in any method which might save threatened species. From him I learned that although it was the aim of his Society to breed endangered animals within their natural habitat, up to date this had only been achieved with the European Eagle Owl. They were re-introduced to Germany and Sweden where they had become extinct. The possibility of breeding mammalian predators, and in particular the great cats of Africa, under natural conditions was he believed at present still a Utopian ideal. I then pointed out that Elsa and Pippa had already proved that such a Utopian ideal could be realized and suggested that if these, the greatest of predators, could thus be saved, saving the rest of the endangered mammals would be comparatively easy – provided one could raise the necessary funds and find people to do the work.

The more I realized how urgent it was that this new method of breeding endangered animals under natural conditions should be known and put into practice, the more frustrated I became at having to spend so long in England and thereby miss those most important last few months of my association with Pippa and her cubs. In particular, I was interested to know whether the two males would leave Pippa sooner than Somba, and whether they might all become sexually attracted to each other.

Meanwhile I had to undergo a most complicated operation which needed all the skill of the best surgeon in that field. During the time I was in hospital, a nurse brought me a catalogue promoting a forthcoming exhibition of some of my paintings showing the Kenya Africans in their traditional costumes. This was a great surprise to me. As soon as I was mobile again, I visited it and then during the month that my paintings were on view helped in various ways to make the show successful.

The Exhibition coincided with the publication of my book on Pippa, *The Spotted Sphinx*, and I was glad to be able to help also with its promotion, even though this entailed almost daily interviews, broadcasts and TV appearances. I also worked on the editing of a children's book *Pippa the Cheetah and her Cubs* as well as carrying on negotiations with various film companies to produce, as a TV programme, the cine footage which I had accumulated during the four years I had lived with the cheetah. The force that drove me to undertake all this was my wish to support the Elsa Wild Animal Appeal which was to benefit from these activities. In addition I had meetings with my London trustees and carried on a correspondence with the directors of the Elsa Wild Animal Appeal in the USA; all this would certainly have kept me busily occupied until October, which was the time estimated by my doctor to be needed for my treatment to be completed.

9. Pippa between Life and Death

In spite of all this activity, like the proverbial drop that erodes the hardest rock, my gnawing worries about Pippa and her cubs finally became so unbearable that I suddenly broke off all further treatment, cancelled my engagements, and took the first plane back to Kenya. I arrived in Nairobi on the 7th of September.

I had to wait there for three harassing days before Ben turned up to drive me to Meru. He said the cheetah had been missing during this time and, as it had appeared from their spoor that Pippa had deserted the cubs, he had wanted to find the family before leaving for Nairobi.

When on the 11th of September we at last drove into camp, we went straight off in search of the family, whom Local had fed earlier in the day. But I had to wait until next morning before I spotted Pippa coming from the Gambo plain to the road near the new headquarters. She purred instantly when I walked up to her and, licking my hand and rubbing her silky head against me, seemed as happy as I was.

Meanwhile, the cubs caught up with their mother. They had grown so much that I had difficulty in identifying them. All looked superbly fit; Big Boy and Tiny were much larger than Pippa and Somba, who were of equal size. They were inquisitive enough, although they kept their distance and dodged at once if I made even the slightest move towards them. I asked Ben to fetch the meat and milk from camp, and then walked with the cheetah a few hundred yards off the road to settle near a fallen tree. The cubs immediately took possession of it, prodding each other for the best position on the branches, under which Pippa and I sat together. While I went on caressing her, she purred and purred, and all the four long months of separation seemed forgotten by us both, but not by Somba. Edging carefully towards us, she settled at the other side of Pippa as close to her as I was. I kept on stroking Pippa, partly to assure Somba that I was no danger to her mother, which Pippa's purring confirmed. Gradually Somba inched herself into such a position that I could not avoid stroking her when I stroked Pippa; thus she kept on pretending not to be interested in me but at the same time making friends. Big Boy and Tiny joined us. Tiny purred and looked at me for a long time with his dark, soft eyes but the moment I moved my hand towards him he rolled out of reach. Big Boy seemed indifferent to my patting him but he never purred. So we sat, all together, utterly content. I felt sublimely happy as I could not have asked for a more wonderful welcome.

When Ben appeared with the food the cheetah were so thirsty that they nearly upset the milk before I could pour it into the bowl. Instantly Somba and Tiny buried their heads in it – pushing Big Boy and Pippa away so that they had to lap from the water-can. There was only a little meat left from the last goat, and even that was high. Despite this the cheetah ate it all to the last scrap and wanted more. So Ben went to fetch a new goat. He told me that this might take some time since he had – at the Warden's request – moved the herd on the 1st of October from Kenmare to Local's home outside the Park. The distance was twenty-two miles, which made it difficult to have the meat available when it was needed.

After he had left the cubs started to play. Chasing each other across the recently burnt ground, they stirred up such clouds of ash that I could not take any photographs. I tried to join Pippa who rested under a tree a short distance away, but when I approached her she moved on, calling the cubs, and all walked off in the direction they had come from. Watching them disappear, I suddenly noticed that Pippa had a slight limp.

As Ben had taken the Land-Rover to get a goat, Local and I had to walk the three miles home. By then it was midday and very hot. After plodding on for a while I spotted the family through the field-glasses; they were resting under a bush, licking each other, and rolling on to their backs with their paws stretched up to catch the slightest breeze in the simmering heat. I was torn between a wish to spend the whole day with them and the risk that they might follow us back to camp if we now joined them. Hoping to act in their best interest, we made a long detour and, looking back repeatedly to watch if they came after us, I was glad to see that they were far too sleepy to move.

When we arrived in camp at lunchtime, George was waiting for me. His news was sad. I knew already from his letters that he had had trouble with the Park Authorities about his lions, and now he had been asked to leave his camp. This was distressing enough, but even more so because of Sandie. The little cub had been seen on and off in the company of George's pride, but had on a few occasions turned up alone near the camp, very hungry. Sandie was only six months old and far too young to survive alone. In the hope of keeping an eye on her, at least from a distance, George had suggested to the Warden that he move into my camp and otherwise remain as a tourist in the Park. He was now waiting for the Warden's reply. His worries about Sandie had been his reason for not meeting me at the airport in Nairobi, and even now he was in a hurry to get home in case Sandie might show up at his camp.

As soon as he had left, Ben turned up with a goat and the news that Local's wife, who herded the goats, was very ill and had to be taken to the hospital. As there was only Ben to drive her there, I agreed that he and Local should take her at once to the Mission Hospital high up in the Jombeni hills so that they could be back again by dark. Unfortunately this meant that Pippa's family would get no more meat that day since it was not safe for Stanley and myself to go through the bush without a rifle, for which only Ben and Local had a licence. But as we had seen several herds of Grant and waterbuck on our way from Pippa to the camp, I hoped that she would kill one of these if she were hungry.

Early next morning we returned to where we had left the family, but found no trace of them, nor did we see any vultures to guide us to a kill. We searched in vain for the following two days and did not even find a spoor.

On the 15th of September Ben took the Land-Rover for repair to Meru, and so I was again alone in camp. Exhausted from the long, hot walk to find the cheetah, I poured myself a Cinzano at sundown to celebrate the publication of Pippa's book on that day. But where was my Spotted Sphinx? There was no reason to be depressed as the family had often been absent for a few days – all the same I could not help feeling that something had gone wrong.

As soon as Ben returned, we split up into two's in order to cover more ground in our search; Ben carrying a rifle went with Stanley, and Local with his rifle searched with me. From dawn to dusk we screened all possible places without finding a trace except that after three days Ben saw a dark-coloured cheetah on the road between the camp and 'Mile 5'. From his description it sounded like Pippa's mate. He had not been near camp since he had sired Pippa's present cubs, and I wondered if they had been together again.

George had promised to help us track, and so at lunchtime the next day we drove to his camp. On the way we noticed several baboons perched high up in a leafless tree, staring at the ground. It seemed odd that they should expose themselves to the midday heat. I drove the car nearer until we saw a lioness under the tree clutching a dead baboon; she must have killed it just before we arrived because the body was still unopened. To save the besieged baboons the gruesome spectacle of watching their pal being eaten, I drove the car right up to the lioness, who quickly straddled her quarry between her legs and dragged it to a nearby river. Instantly the baboons dropped off the tree and, racing away, were joined by more baboons who had been watching from distant trees.

Late next afternoon we found a single cheetah spoor, which looked like Pippa's, on the Kenmare road within half a mile of my camp. It turned towards the rivulet where we lost it on the overgrown bank. Early next morning, Ben went with Local to follow up this spoor, while I remained in camp in case Pippa turned up. A little later Ben returned, breathless. He had found Pippa only 300 yards away, lying under a tree with a broken leg. Rushing after him, I saw her hobbling on three legs, the left front leg dangling limp from her shoulder. Every few yards she collapsed, staggered to her feet, and dragged herself on until she fell again. Thus she reached the tree under which her cub had been buried. There she lay down, utterly exhausted. Quickly I gave her milk, the only food I had for her in camp, which she drank non-stop. She was terribly thin and looked very ill. I sent Ben off to get a goat, and asked him on his way through Leopard Rock to try and radio-call a vet. I knew that the Harthoorns were at present in South Africa, but there were the two vets that Tony had recommended and I hoped that one of them would be willing to come – even though today was Sunday.

I then tried to entice Pippa into Whity's compound by showing her the meat basket. Trustingly, she staggered after it. I hated fooling her like this but it was essential that she should be got into a confined space as soon as possible. Hoping to comfort her, I caressed her, but whenever I touched her she growled, obviously she was in great pain. She had been missing for nine days and, judging from her emaciated condition, she could not have eaten for at least a week. If she had been near to camp at the time of the accident we would have found traces of the cubs; so I feared that the injury had happened a long way from here and that poor Pippa must have suffered agonizing pain in covering the distance to find help in camp.

How glad I was that I was here. My abrupt departure from London now seemed almost to have been due to second sight, and my strange foreboding on the day of the publication of *The Spotted Sphinx* had proved tragically justified.

When Ben arrived with a goat we gave Pippa the thorax; she gulped it down so ravenously that she brought it all up again. Utterly spent and worn out, she then fell asleep.

Ben had not been able to get through on the radio; so we decided that he should drive to Nairobi at once to get a vet. I could not spare my only car in case of an emergency arising so I hoped that George would lend us one of his three Land-Rovers. We arranged that, during the time it would take for me to drive to George to get the car, Ben would search with Local for the cubs and retrace Pippa's spoor. Unfortunately they found no sign of the cubs, but Pippa's spoor came from the plains where she had given birth to Whity, Mbili and Tatu, some three miles from the camp, and led farther still towards the Murera-Golo Circuit.

At teatime Ben left for Nairobi and, all being well, I calculated that he would be there by midnight. I spent the afternoon with Pippa, feeding her small pieces of meat, but she was very weak and slept most of the time. In the evening the Warden called and we discussed the situation. Pippa would need help for some time to come. I knew that Tony Harthoorn was, in principle, against removing a wild animal from its natural habitat unless absolutely essential, because it had been proved that for wild animals the need to adapt themselves to unfamiliar surroundings was so harmful that veterinary help in hospitals couldn't compensate for it. The Warden on the other hand was dead against having an invalid animal in the Park for any length of time. What was I to do?

I spent a sleepless night listening to Pippa's slightest movement in the enclosure next to my hut. Suddenly I heard a snort. Rushing out with my torch, I saw a buffalo grazing on the far bank of the rivulet; blinded by the light-beam he thundered off. Soon after this Pippa gave the low moan she always uttered when she was worried about the cubs. Hoping to get a glimpse of them, I dashed out again and screened the surroundings with the flashlight, but saw nothing. As soon as it was light I sent Local off to search for the cubs by tracing their spoor. He found that they had slept near the place where the buffalo had been grazing. Their spoor then led to the 'Kill Acacia' and farther to plains beyond which he lost them. So evidently Pippa had called to the cubs when they had been frightened by the buffalo whom I had seen off by the glare of my torch.

While Local continued searching for them I sat with Pippa, waiting for the vet. Assuming that he might have to sedate her for examination, I gave her only a little to eat although she was hungry. She resented my sitting close to her, which showed how ill she was. I respected her wish to be left alone and sat outside the enclosure typing letters, which gave me an excuse to watch her all the time without infringing on her privacy.

Remembering Pippa's slight limp nine days ago, I felt remorse at not having taken meat to her that afternoon, because I had thereby forced her in her handicapped state to kill a buck which might have been too big for her. She had a patch of abraided skin above the elbow, which could have been caused by the kick of a hoofed animal. I had often been worried about her preference for waterbuck, which are one of the more common antelopes here but, unless immature, are far too large a prey for cheetah. It was more than I could bear now to see Pippa with such a terrible injury – as well as to think of what might happen to her poor cubs.

I was glad when George turned up for lunch to comfort me and to help Local in searching for the cubs. At 3 p.m. an aircraft landed at Kenmare, bringing a vet, Ben and the pilot. While I collected the party, George returned to camp without having found the cubs.

Having seen Pippa so irritable that morning, I wondered if the vet would be able to examine her without sedating her;

need not have worried, as she allowed him to handle her without the slightest resistance. She had reacted in just this way to a vet two years ago, whose manipulation she had tolerated although he was unknown to her. I was convinced that on both occasions she knew that these strangers wanted to help her.

The verdict was grave. The leg seemed to be broken below the elbow and the fracture was so bad that the vet wanted to destroy Pippa there and then. I pleaded for a chance to save her. Reluctantly he agreed but insisted on taking her at once to Nairobi for an X-ray and possible treatment. Before anaesthetizing her for the trip, he asked me to sign my agreement for him to destroy her should he find it necessary. I had no choice but to sign if I wanted to save Pippa's life, but I almost fainted. The vet then injected the anaesthetic, the dose based on the weight of a hundred pound body; Pippa reacted instantly. He then tied her legs and put on a muzzle so tight that Pippa threw two fits, during which her tongue protruded between her firmly tied lips. Fearing that she might bite through her tongue in a convulsion I begged to have the rope loosened a little, but he insisted on this measure as he had previously been mauled by a cheetah under similar circumstances. I hoped that I could fly with Pippa to Nairobi by taking Ben's seat – but the vet preferred me to stay behind and Ben went instead.

Before the plane took off at 5 p.m., we arranged that I should drive with George straight to Nairobi so that I could be with Pippa, and that Ben should return early next morning with George's Land-Rover and look after the cubs while I was away.

Watching a plane disappear into space with an injured animal inside it has always been a heartbreak; this time I felt as if the last drop of blood would drain from me, but there was no time to lose and I packed up my kit, ready to start immediately. George however was worried about Sandie and would not leave till next morning. I spent the night at his

camp and we drove off at dawn. On the way we met Ben, returning. He told us that Pippa had been so ill on her arrival
that the vet had wondered whether she would survive. He had
weighed her and had found that in her emaciated state, the
scales had shown only seventy-one pounds compared with a
healthy cheetah's body weight of a hundred pounds. No
wonder poor Pippa had reacted so violently to the anaesthetizing overdose. At the hospital the vet had vaccinated her
against feline enteritis and put the broken leg into a plaster-
cast. After she had been bedded on hay Pippa had settled
down, and when Ben saw her that morning she seemed a little
better. Much relieved, I asked him to write me daily news of
the cubs.

By 3 p.m. I was with Pippa in the hospital section of the
Animal Orphanage. She had not come round from the anaesthetic, and her leg was in plaster from the shoulder down-
wards. Her pen was about 5 ft by 8 ft, adjoining similar-sized
enclosures, with four cheetah cubs in one and a young duiker
in the other. Opposite was a larger pen containing five cheetah
cubs. All nine cubs had been recently found abandoned and
were now kept here for observation after being vaccinated
against feline enteritis. There were also five tiny lion cubs
with mangy skins who had been found without a mother. All
these animals were housed in the headquarters' building of the
original orphanage which had been converted into an animal
hospital after a better orphanage had recently been built. Both
establishments belong to the Kenya National Parks and were
situated right and left of the main entrance gate. Visitors were
encouraged to see the inhabitants in the new orphanage, where
the animals were detained until they could be released, but
they were not permitted to disturb the sick animals who were
kept in outdoor paddocks on the old orphanage site, let alone
enter the hospital.

We called on the Director of the Kenya National Parks,
Perez Olindo, who was an old friend of mine. Hearing of
Pippa's predicament, he was very sympathetic and offered his

help. We also knew the Warden of the orphanage, Julian Tong, well enough to ask if I could stay with him and his wife as a paying guest so that I could live as close to Pippa as possible. They kindly agreed and, before George returned to Meru, I was installed at their home a few miles away.

Next morning I found Pippa still dopey, but not sufficiently sedated to stop her from being irritated by the plaster cast. In her efforts to get rid of this unwieldy burden she threw herself around in violent spasms, jumping high against the walls and crashing to the ground at such precarious angles that I was terrified of her breaking her neck. The pen was much too small for me to calm her down when she was in such a frantic state, and so I was extremely glad when the vet arrived and agreed that she should be moved into the bigger pen, the one which was at the moment occupied by the five cheetah cubs. Julian very kindly helped to clean the place thoroughly, and arranged that enough bales of hay should always be available to keep Pippa comfortably bedded. The vet predicted that she would have to be in plaster for at least three weeks, and would then need to be kept confined for a further three weeks to strengthen the leg. She had to be under constant observation during this period; needed to be turned over every two hours to prevent her from getting pneumonia and besides this someone had to see that she was covered during the chilly nights, and that her pen was kept spotlessly clean. For all these reasons it was agreed that I should sleep next to Pippa, not only so that I could nurse her by day and by night, but so that she would also have somebody familiar near her during this strange and distressing time.

We organized ample supplies of meat, eggs, milk, glucose and vitamins, apart from the medications which the vet provided daily. Julian, most thoughtfully, brought a mattress and bedding for me; he also offered to bring my food along each morning and suggested that I should have a bath at his home during the midday lull when Pippa would be sleeping.

Meanwhile she had to be under sedation all the time to keep her quiet and make her pain bearable. She still had a temperature, and an ice-cold nose, and lived only on glucose, eggs and milk. I bought two cotton sheets for her to lie on, which I washed as soon as one was wetted, and I changed the hay so that no fleas or smell could foul her pen. I also bought a small folding table and chair so that I could type letters outside her pen when she was asleep. During most of the time during the first days, I had to hold her down whenever she began to thresh hoping to free herself from the uncomfortable splint. After each 'fight' between us, she licked my hands, which only a few moments before had been gripping her firmly to prevent additional injuries and thus seemed to thank me for helping her. She also purred sometimes during the treatments which the vet came twice a day to administer.

As soon as she was better, she answered the chirpings of the cheetah cubs who called for their mothers. I would have given anything to understand their chatterings – it was obvious that they derived comfort from each other in spite of their not being able to see Pippa. Once she heaved herself up to the windowsill and, looking through the glass, discovered two bears who were kept in a paddock opposite the hospital. These were the only non-African animals here and they greatly intrigued her. Thereafter I had to support her every morning in an upright position so that she could watch them, otherwise she would have struggled on her own to reach the windowsill and would have harmed herself.

After four days she no longer had a temperature; ate well and not only purred whenever I fed her, but often uttered a soft 'Nyam, Nyam, Nyam' – a sound which I had only previously heard from Whity when expressing happiness while feeding. She had given it when she too had been confined with a broken leg. Pippa's condition improved so much that the vet thought it safe to go away for the weekend, but he gave me the address of another vet to contact in an emergency.

Next morning Pippa was in a most irritable mood. Licking

the upper edge of the splint, she insisted on keeping the broken leg on top whenever I tried to turn her over. I took her temperature – it was 104° F. Alarmed, I called the second vet who gave her an antibiotic at 10 a.m. and asked me to call him again should her temperature go on rising – but he added that he would only be available until lunchtime.

At 3 p.m. Pippa's temperature climbed up to 105° F. By a lucky coincidence, a veterinary chemist whom I knew arrived just then to visit the sick animals at the hospital. He sniffed at Pippa's leg – it stank. He then pressed the plaster cast until pus oozed out from underneath. Very kindly, he telephoned every vet within reach, but it was a Sunday and it was 5 p.m. before he found a vet at home. His arrival coincided with the return of Pippa's first vet who had come back from his week-end trip sooner than he had anticipated. After anaesthetizing her the two vets removed the plaster cast. The leg, from the elbow to the toes, was gangrenous, and there was also a large hole filled with pus where the edge of the splint had chafed the shoulder during Pippa's attempts to tear it off. The hair, which still covered a few places on the leg, came off like cotton wool as soon as it was touched. Both vets regarded her case as hopeless for the circulation of blood had stopped; the leg was dead, and within three days at the latest, all the flesh would wither and the bones rot away. Both suggested destroying her instantly. Panic-stricken, I insisted on having the opinion of yet one more vet. He was not available until the next day.

Meanwhile Pippa was kept under heavy sedation and injected with antibiotics. In spite of this, she had a very bad night, during which I changed her bandages four times.

My hope was now pinned on the fourth vet. When he turned up around midday, he made a thorough examination and told me he believed the leg could be saved, but he warned me that Pippa might never recover its full use. I had seen several wild animals – including predators – surviving in the wild on three legs, or with only one eye, and even if Pippa would never be able to hunt again, she could be an invaluable link in helping me to rehabilitate more cheetah and perhaps enjoy another ten years of living semi-wild.

After consulting the first vet, both vets agreed to work together – the original vet would visit Pippa in the morning, while the fourth and latest vet would come in the late afternoon; both leaving notes for each other about their treatment. The fourth then started dressing the wound with furocin ointment, and he prescribed kaolin poultices to draw out the infection and prevent further gangrene contamination.

A grim routine developed. Vet 1 called at 8 a.m. to inspect the wound and sedate Pippa for the day. Although I greatly appreciated his co-operation, knowing that it was against his principles to keep an animal alive who was as badly injured as poor Pippa was, his pessimistic outlook had a very demoralizing effect on me. After his visits I would feed Pippa with raw meat, eggs and milk; warm up the poultices every ten minutes and change the dressing; give frequent injections or enemas with a solution of glucose and salt to prevent dehydration; administer medicines for her digestion (which was often upset due to the sedatives); keep the syringe clean; wash the sheets repeatedly and scrub the pen. Between these chores I sat with Pippa, stroking and brushing her, which she liked. Sometimes she uttered a heart-rending moan, calling her cubs, and in her semi-conscious state would stare at me with widely dilated pupils until she recognized me and relaxed.

After tea, Vet 4 would come to treat her wounds, control her heart with medicines, and then sedate her for the night. He shared my faith in Pippa's recovery. Aided by her remarkable resilience and the best medicines, we both hoped to pull her through the present crisis.

The nights were often a great ordeal. Resting at ground level next to Pippa, I could hear even her faintest groan, which often preceded a convulsion that would shake her body to the point of exhaustion. Even if I held her and tried thus to diminish the cramp which I could feel rippling through her from head to tail, she often tore the bandage off during these rages, and I had to disinfect the wounds quickly and dress them again. When she had one of her rare spells of rest the cries of the sick animals in the adjoining pens made sleep impossible for me, and I waited for the crowing of a cock, which usually happened at 5 a.m., soon after which the hospital staff would knock at the door to start a new day's routine.

During the long, sleepless hours, I thought of a way in which I could show my gratitude to the people here for helping Pippa in so many ways, and for allowing me to stay with her day and night. Having had access to the medical store, and seen the very limited supply they had, I decided to set up a fund in Pippa's name to provide sufficient medicines for the treatment of wild animals here, or wherever it was needed in the bush. This would entail planning with the trustees of the Elsa Wild Animal Appeal and I made up my mind to discuss my scheme with them as soon as possible.

The suffering of animals has always been a torment to me, but how much more acute was it now, when anxiety for Pippa keyed up my nerves to breaking point. In particular the cries of pain of one of the small lion cubs were more than I could bear. At night I watched it circling round and round with lowered head, until it fell down burying its nose into the hay, nearly suffocating. Whenever Pippa had a few calm moments, I took the poor cub into my lap and tried to comfort it, until it again started racing round in circles. Four nights the poor little creature struggled on, then it died. It was most distressing to watch it being carried away, together with a young duiker, a reed-buck fawn and two cheetah, who had also succumbed to their illnesses that night. Despite such heartbreaking cases, my faith became stronger day by day that Pippa might recover. I saw her eating well, her wound gradually becoming cleaner and no longer smelly; even the circulation had returned to most parts of her leg. It seemed almost a miracle to watch her getting better every day. Now, if her bones could be kept healthy and her heart stood up to all the heavy sedatives, she would be safe.

The more she improved, the less could I understand why the first vet continued to regard my persistence in keeping her alive as selfishness if not sadistic cruelty. He believed the treatment to be an absolute waste of time and had lately refused to take Pippa's temperature saying she was dying anyway, but, however upsetting his visits might be to me, he continued his morning calls as the other vet did not have the time to drive eight miles to the orphanage twice a day in order to sedate Pippa in the morning.

Meanwhile the news of Pippa's accident had got around, and friends came offering to baby-sit so that now and then I could have a bath; they also lent me their car to drive to Julian's house, and brought me titbits and cutlery to make my life as comfortable as they could.

Amongst the new friends I made was Lew Hurxthal, a student of Zoology from the USA. He came to thank me for having got a grant from the Elsa Wild Animal Appeal to help him to study ostrich in the Nairobi National Park. Since his term at the university had not yet started, he offered to do shopping for me or run errands.

One day my friend and doctor, Gerald Nevill, visited me. He was concerned about my hand and insisted that a physiotherapist should treat it right here at the hospital. Although the operation in London had been a success, the hand was getting stiff and clawing up because the skin and bones had adhered to the transplanted tendon. Consequently, the fingers could not pull out. He recommended that I should wear a splint at least during the night to straighten the hand, but that I could not do for I had a full-time job with, at the most, five hours' sleep at odd times and I could not be handicapped by a cumbersome splint.

Meanwhile, the healing of Pippa's leg progressed and she was now in more danger from the sedatives she constantly had to take, than from her injuries. How long could her heart stand up to these powerful drugs? The afternoon vet injected liver and heart stimulants, and simultaneously reduced the dosage of the sedatives, and told me to give her more only if it were absolutely essential.

The following night Pippa started to growl at eleven o'clock, and soon went into such long and rigid cramps that I had to inject the remaining sedative, after which she slept well. Next morning her temperature was below normal. The afternoon vet was very concerned about her heart, so he tried a different sedative – RO-5-2807, plus Acetylpromazin with only a little Sernylan – he expected the new sedative to have less exhausting side-effects than did the full dose of Sernylan plus Acetylpromazin which he had used up to now. Again he injected a minimum dose and left the rest for me to give only if necessary.

I also nearly became one of his patients. Earlier in the day I had burnt my right hand with boiling water and the blisters were now bursting. He was anxious that these open wounds should not be infected when I dressed Pippa's leg, and insisted that a doctor be called to give me penicillin as well as a tetanus injection. By the time the doctor arrived at 8 p.m. we were literally in the dark because of an electricity shortage at the hospital. So we had to get the night-watchman to open the office of the National Park, and there the doctor treated me. As soon as I had received the two pricks, I took up my vigil again next to Pippa in the dark.

She was weak, and breathed very slowly, but remained calm all night and needed no additional sedatives. Listening anxiously to her breathing, I suddenly heard a faint chirp, like the call of a young cheetah cub. There was still no light in the hospital so I couldn't discover its origin. I was puzzled – all the cheetah cubs had been moved away from here a few days ago to the new orphanage. But as this was unmistakably the call of a young cub, the newcomer must have arrived while I was having the injections. Holding Pippa close to me and feeling her very slow heart beat, the repeated calling of this cheetah cub upset me.

By next morning, Pippa's breathing was normal, but her temperature was still only 100° F. I mentioned this to the morning vet, who was exceptionally friendly today. While watching me feeding Pippa half a pound of meat, he injected RO-5-2807 plus the full dose Sernylan sedatives. I then offered Pippa more meat, but she closed her eyes and her head sank down. I asked why she had stopped eating, the vet replied that perhaps she was tired, and left.

Pippa never woke up again. It was the 7th of October.

Later in the morning Lew Hurxthal called and kindly offered to drive us to Meru so that Pippa could be buried at her camp. He then left to make a wooden box for her; bought dry ice to wrap her in, and hired a Land-Rover since the large heavy box would not fit into a charter plane. Meanwhile, I sent a radio message to George, asking him to meet us next afternoon with digging implements at Pippa's camp.

When we carried Pippa out of the hospital, I was haunted by the chirping of the new cheetah cub, who went on calling, calling, and calling, as we drove off.

On the long drive to Meru I had ample time to reflect on all that had happened during the last seventeen days. It was too late now to know that Pippa might have been saved if a light, metal splint, or better still, a plastic one, had been fixed to her leg so that a daily examination of her wound would have been possible. By using a detachable splint, Pippa could have remained at Meru inside Whity's compound where she would have been in familiar surroundings and her fretting at having to be confined would have been reduced to a minimum.

It seemed strange that history was repeating itself, that Pippa, like Elsa, had to die while both their cubs were just, but only just, old enough to survive alone.

I could hardly wait to hear the latest news of Tiny, Big Boy and Somba. Ben had written that on the 23rd of September, the day I had left Meru, the cubs had been seen by the Warden on the new airstrip; fit, and with full bellies.

During the following week, the men had found several cheetah spoor, and the bones of a young waterbuck with cheetah tracks around. But it had taken nine days before they came upon the cubs on a ridge about two miles behind the new headquarters. Guided by a vulture to the remains of a duiker, they spotted them a few yards away under a bush. When Ben approached them, they purred and seemed happy at seeing him again after twenty days – the last time at which we had all been together.

After half-an-hour Tiny got up, followed by Big Boy and finally by Somba, and all walked away slowly through the very dense bush. Whenever Tiny stopped, the others stopped; when Tiny went on, they did so too. It seemed as if he had taken over the leadership from Big Boy; nevertheless he was the shyest when Ben attempted to touch him – the others did not seem to mind. So they all strolled on until it became too hot and they sat down. Later the men returned to camp for lunch, but at teatime brought milk and found the trio still resting under the same tree. Somba had tolerated Ben playing with her, until it got dark. Since then they had seen no trace of the cubs for eight days.

It was late afternoon when we reached camp. George and the men had already prepared the grave for Pippa next to the little cairn under which her son was buried. Both were overshadowed by the tree where she and her families had so often played, while watching everything that was going on in camp. By the silence with which the men welcomed Pippa home I knew how much her death meant to them.

We lowered her into the pit, but before covering the box with earth I placed three small stones on it as a symbol for Tiny, Big Boy and Somba, hoping that they might comfort each other. We then put Pippa to rest. It was strange how calm I suddenly felt. It was of immense importance to me that Pippa rested here in her own world, for I knew that she would now continue to be with us and give me strength to carry out all I wanted to do in her name.

10. Reunion with the Cubs

The most urgent task now was to find Pippa's cubs. The men had followed their spoor in the morning, coming from the Rojoweru bridge along the road for two miles, and ending near the new airstrip, where they had lost them.

In order to save time, they left early the next day to continue their search, while I unpacked. But I had hardly started sorting things out when a party of visitors from the USA arrived, wanting my autograph and their photograph taken with me. I was quite used to such invasions by strangers who regarded my life in camp as a public enterprise and showed no respect for privacy. As often as I could I met the demands of the intruders, but today I felt I could not cope with them and explained the situation to their guide. Seeing my red and swollen eyes, and the newly dug grave, they might have left me alone, but instead they settled down for a merry chat, persistently focusing their cameras on me and pressing me for a 'good smile'.

At midday the men returned without news of the cubs. After lunch, Local and Stanley carried on where they had left the spoors, and George and I searched in different directions, while Ben drove with Lew Hurxthal some thirty miles to the Adamson Falls on the Tana River. There we knew there were large granite slabs piled up along the rapids and polished smooth by the torrent. These would I thought make a fine surface for Pippa's grave.

For the next few days, we repeated this teamwork but found no sign of the cubs. Meanwhile we erected a large cairn of rough stone-work which we covered with the Tana slabs. When Lew had to return to Nairobi, he took the best piece with him to get Pippa's name and dates engraved. Later we

placed it on the centre of the cairn, cemented all the slabs together so that no elephant could damage it, and finally cleared
a large circle free of grass around the graves of Pippa and
her son. His little cairn was sheltered by Pippa's large one.
By building such elaborate graves for Elsa and Pippa I risked
being accused of morbid tendencies. Nevertheless I wanted
to honour both these animals for letting me share their lives
and for all they had done to give human beings hope of
making our world as good as theirs.

George had recently been given permission to remain in
the Park, and to move into my camp. As soon as he had
arrived with his belongings we saw a cloud of smoke rising
in the direction where, until an hour ago, he had made his
home for the last four years. We were silent – there was no
need of words. I felt so sorry for George.

Ben had left with Lew Hurxthal for two weeks, saying that
'a holiday would do him good'. This unfortunately meant that
we would not be able to cover as much ground as we could
have, had there been two parties searching for the cubs. The
weather was very hot and tracking all day long was exhausting.
I could only avoid headaches by plunging, fully, dressed, into
the rivulets along which we often searched, and repeating this
cooling system as soon as I had walked myself dry. I only
realized now how much had depended on Pippa's liaison between us and her children, and that they had merely tolerated
our presence because she wished them to do so. I felt certain that they were sometimes within hearing distance, but
there was never a response to my calls as we plodded on day
after day.

Twice we found a single cheetah spoor, and close to this we
saw the dark male – Pippa's mate perhaps – crossing the road
again within a mile of camp and disappearing towards the
Mulika. Hoping that he might give us a clue as to the cubs'
whereabouts, we followed his tracks, only to run into two
lions which made any further search in that area futile.

One day, we came upon a dead elephant cow. The hard,

dried skin still covered part of the body, and both her tusks were lying within a few inches of her head. This indicated that she must have died a natural death. Less lucky had been a giraffe, which we found within a mile of the Park boundary. Its tail had been cut off – perhaps to make a fly-whisk with? – and part of the skin had been severed by knives, obviously the work of poachers.

On one occasion we were walking through the bush, concentrating on tracking, when we almost ran into two lions on a buffalo kill, deeply absorbed in their feast. We were all taken by surprise and, luckily, the lions bolted. Knowing that George would like to find out if these lions were his charges, we went back to camp to collect him. During the five hours it took us to return the lions had filled their bellies to bursting point, and were resting near the kill. But the younger lion rushed over to it several times to thwart the vultures who loaded the surrounding trees, waiting for their turn. There were Ruppell's Griffon vultures, white-and-pink-necked ones, and of course the never-failing marabou storks. After George had driven close enough to know that these two lions were not members of his pride, we left the party to their feast and went on searching in that area for Pippa's cubs. When we passed by the buffalo kill again on our return about an hour later, there was no sign of the two lions, but all the vultures had coalesced into a feather heap, treading on top of each other, and tearing off the last edible sinews from the almost bare bones.

I was interested to notice that the marabou now had their pouches inflated, as I was certain they had been at normal size when they were previously perching on the trees. There are many theories which try to explain when and why these pouches, which extend from the front of their neck, become air-filled, but so far none has proved satisfactory.

The rains were not far off and it was time to burn the grass again. Since the Warden did not have enough staff to do this in the more remote areas, he gladly accepted my offer to set some of the plains alight on our searches. This especially concerned the country between the tributaries of the Rojoweru which we knew thoroughly by now. Watching the wind carefully one morning, we had hardly started throwing matches on the plain between two of these rivulets, when the strawy grass burst into flame all around us at such incredible speed that we had to run for our lives to the rivulet, reaching it only just in time to plunge headlong in, to escape the raging fire behind us. Climbing up the far bank, we found ourselves in extremely thick thornbush carpeted with rhino and buffalo droppings, and heard these animals snorting and crashing through the wood all around us. It was a hellish situation as we would have had no hope of running away should we have met these living tanks face to face. To add to this unpleasant situation I found I had a deep gash on my shin which I had cut when jumping into the river, and the blood was now trickling uncomfortably into my boot. But before I could attend to it we had to concentrate on getting out of this twisted mass before the fire might jump the rivulet and we would be trapped. When we finally emerged on to more open ground we nearly collided with a sleeping rhino. It so strikingly resembled a termite hill that we nearly stepped on it before it got up, swerved round and, with an angry snort, crashed into the thorny hell from which we had just escaped. Looking at my bleeding scratches I envied the beast its pachydermous skin, but not its favourite habitat.

When Ben returned, we were again able to split up into two's and search in different directions. But days and days went by without a sign of our trio. As if to mock us, there were now two single cheetah in Pippa's territory, one near Kenmare and one along the Rojoweru near the airstrip; tracking after their spoor misled us for several days until we caught sight of them and saw that they were not Pippa's cubs.

The rains had started and often made tracking impossible. Things became still more complicated when Ben developed knee-cap trouble from an old injury; it needed urgent treatment in Nairobi. While we were filling up with petrol at the new headquarters for his trip, we were told that early in the morning, Pippa's cubs had been seen near the waterpump about half a mile away. And sure enough, there we found the pugmarks of all three cubs. With our eyes glued to the stony ground we traced the imprints, step by step, for about an hour, calling Pippa's name, then I spotted a Lesser Kudu running. As I watched this beautiful antelope through my field-glasses I was suddenly conscious of being watched myself, and, looking round, saw Tiny, Somba and Big Boy peeping at me through the grass only a few feet away. Had they been stalking this Kudu? They were obviously hungry. We gave them the milk we always carried with us, which they drank thirstily, pushing their heads together into the small bowl as they had done since they were tiny cubs. I could now see how much they had grown in the last weeks, and in what excellent condition they were. Ben offered to go with Stanley to collect a goat, so that I could meanwhile enjoy our reunion.

I followed the cubs to a shady tree, Local keeping a short distance behind, and we all sat down. Tiny and Big Boy soon dozed off in the midday heat, but Somba kept alert to the slightest movement, and shifted instantly away if I tried to inch nearer to her. Of course the cubs had not seen me for more than six months, with the exception of that morning, forty-six days ago, when Pippa had been for the last time to-gether with us all. It was now twenty-five days since Ben had found the cubs at their duiker kill. Although I had known that they were already able to hunt on their own I had often despaired in the last weeks, and had wondered if they were still alive. Only an hour ago I had prayed, asking that we would find them fit – and now my prayer had been answered.

The peace around us was a wonderful anti-climax to the tension of the past weeks. Why is it that only animals give me this feeling of utter content with nothing lacking? My happiness would have been absolute if Pippa had still been with us. But even if she were no longer physically present, I felt her very close, and believed that she had helped us to find her cubs. Certainly they had responded when I called her name. This was significant, and I decided from now on to use her name as a link between the cubs and myself.

Each one of them carried on some endearing part of her. Big Boy had taken over her loving care of the family; licking his brother and sister affectionately, he reassured them until they snuggled up to him as they had done with Pippa. Tiny had all her charm and trusting sincerity, while Somba guarded the family against the slightest danger and thus protected them with motherly anxiety.

Suddenly, all three sat up and stared into the direction from which Ben and Stanley soon appeared, carrying the carcass of a goat. As soon as the cubs got hold of it, they dragged it under a bush where no vultures could see them eating it. Within half-an-hour there was nothing left except bits of skin, a few bones, and the head. When I attempted to smash this into pulp so that it could be eaten too, Somba defended it at once with lowered head, and struck so rapidly at me with her front legs that I quickly dropped the head. Hoping to divert her interest, I offered her some marrow on a piece of goatskin that Local had extracted from the bones. She did not know what to do with it, but it aroused the curiosity of Tiny. He had always regarded marrow as his privilege, and now made a dash for his favourite titbit; only to be chased instantly by Big Boy who did not wish to miss the fun. Hanging on to the skin in a tug-of-war, and splattering the marrow in all directions, they both growled fiercely until Tiny paraded off with most of the skin while Big Boy carried away the little scrap he had been able to secure. This he dropped into the milk bowl and, to guard his trophy, sat next to it till he got bored, drank all the milk and moved away. A moment later Tiny grabbed the skin and gobbled it up. I was so enchanted by the cubs that I forgot all about the time and stayed on until it became too dark to watch them and we had to go home.

11. The Cubs help to save Boy

Next morning Ben left early for Nairobi, while Local and I found the cheetah on a ridge about a mile from headquarters, not far from where we had left them the day before. After we had fed the trio they moved to a large acacia tree some distance away, where they settled for their midday slumber. Knowing that they would like a second helping later on I followed with the remaining meat and, sitting close to the cubs, took a lot of photographs.

Again I had a strange feeling of being watched and, scrutinizing the surroundings through my field-glasses, I spotted a lion lying in the grass some hundred yards away. He looked straight at me without moving. The little I could see of his body, hidden by the grass, seemed very emaciated, with dark stripes indicating the position of his ribs. I then noticed a porcupine quill protruding from two inches below his eye. Knowing how fatal these quills can be to any predator who hunts the delicious-tasting porcupines I realized that this emaciated lion must have been badly injured and most likely had more quills embedded in his feet, which would make moving very painful, if not impossible.

Meanwhile the cubs were quite oblivious of their neighbour, and crunched away at the meat. How, without alarming them unduly, could I make them leave the area? I signalled Local, who had not yet seen the lion, to come to me. Placing ourselves between the lion and the cheetah, we watched both parties until Tiny became suspicious. Staring at the lion, he uttered a strange, deep growling moan, and was off – with Big Boy and Somba racing after him. I was relieved that they had spotted the lion themselves as I would not have liked to have had to frighten them away while our relationship was still rather delicate.

Repeatedly I now called the names of George's lions Boy and Suswa, but this lion just looked at me without even flicking an ear. I did not know what to make of his behaviour; it was as improbable for a wild animal as for a lion belonging to George's pride. Since I could not leave an injured lion so close to headquarters, I sent Local by a long detour back to the car, while I walked the odd mile to the headquarters to call the Warden. To my surprise, I found George in the Warden's office, both discussing Boy's future. As soon as George heard my story, he became very worried since Boy had been seen limping badly three weeks ago about five miles from here, and had been missing since. When I suggested that this lion might be the victim of porcupine quills, the Warden confirmed that of all the lions he had had to destroy in the past, ninety per cent had been injured by quills. He had pulled sixty quills out of one lioness. Wherever possible he always saved the lives of the unfortunate animals, and he would naturally try to help this lion too, although he took his heavy rifle along in case the lion was already beyond help.

We drove to the acacia tree and found the lion still at the same place. As soon as the Warden stepped out of the car, he growled and hobbled off to a bush a few yards away to hide. We could then see that his right front leg was enormously swollen, in contrast to his pelvis and spine which stuck out so alarmingly that we realized the poor creature must have been on the verge of starvation. George drove his car slowly towards the lion; after a while, he got out and filled the old steel helmet, which had already served as an uncrunchable drinking bowl for Elsa, with water which he then gave the lion. He had left the door of the Land-Rover open, and before he could prevent it the lion clambered inside and sprawled on the seats. By offering him more water, George got him out again and helped him settle down near the familiar water-bowl. He then pulled out the quill and returned to us. Hold-

ing the six-inch quill, George said nothing but 'Boy'. I could
imagine what was going on in George's mind as well as in
that of the Warden, though both kept silent. Since Boy had
mauled the Warden's child, he had suppressed his personal
feelings and had agreed to Boy's remaining in the Park, although he had thrown thunder-flashes at Boy whenever he
had seen him near the headquarters. Here now was a chance
to destroy the lion who had caused so much trouble. There
was a long silence. When the Warden spoke it was to agree to
help Boy. He suggested making a radio-call to Nairobi asking
a vet to fly in and immobilize Boy for a diagnosis. Meanwhile
I collected meat and sulphuthiazole from camp, and George
stayed with Boy.

By the time I returned the Warden had received news that
the vet could not come till the next day. Since we could not
leave Boy alone without the risk of his being attacked by predators, George decided to spend the night with him. While
he collected his kit, as well as another goat, I guarded Boy.
However little I had had to do with him in the last years, he
knew that I was his friend and allowed me to sit within a few
yards of him. Looking at me with unflinching eyes, as he had
done all morning, he trusted me.

Animals sense far better than we humans often can, the true
feelings of other creatures towards them, and though humans
can be fooled by words, animals rely on their thought communication and are never deceived. I was always surprised
when, at the orphanage, the first vet asked me daily if Pippa
had not yet bitten me, and amused to see his astonishment
when I assured him that she always licked my hand and
purred in response to my treatment. Even if I had sometimes
hurt her in the process, she knew that I was trying to help,
and not only co-operated but thanked me. Today Boy had
shown the same trust in George when he allowed him to pull
out one quill and manipulate his swollen leg. Although George
found no further quills he assumed that one or more might be
imbedded deep inside the flesh, causing the leg's distension.

While I sat with Boy I reflected on the extraordinary combination of coincidences which had led to the present situation. First our searches for forty-six days to find the cubs before the rains made spooring very difficult. Then Ben's injured knee, compelling us to buy petrol at the headquarters on the very morning that the cubs had been seen nearby. Then the cubs leading me to Boy, who would certainly have died had I not found him in the nick of time. His injuries must have occurred at least three weeks ago and, obviously, he had dragged himself to the nearest human habitation to find help when he could no longer cope with his handicap – just as Pippa had done. Finally there was the incredible timing of the meeting between the Warden and George, who were both needed at that very hour to save Boy. All these seemed to me to be more than a mere succession of coincidences, but to what purpose – only the future could tell.

George spent an uneventful night with Boy and kept him company until the vet arrived. After sedating Boy he diagnosed a break of the humerus on the right front leg, and a dislocated shoulder. This was the worst combination that could have happened to a right-handed predator. It was now decided between the Warden, the vet and George that Boy should be operated on at George's demolished camp, where the wire-fence was still intact and would provide a secure enclosure. After a three-day confinement there Boy would be let out and George would watch his progress for two weeks. If, after this period, Boy was fit to live completely in the wild again, George was to withdraw; if he had not recovered by then either George would have to remove him from the Park, or he would have to be destroyed.

The vet then returned to Nairobi to collect the instruments needed for such major surgery, and George transported Boy to his former camp. There he rigged up a tent for him while he himself slept nearby inside his Land-Rover. This went on for four days until the vet returned with an assistant. To operate on a lion in the bush had never before been attempted, let alone under such primitive conditions. George had rigged up a canvas shelter underneath which three camp tables served as an operating-table. After Boy had been anaesthetized and heaved on to these tables, the dark bruised areas around his fracture were shaved and disinfected. To enable the vet to concentrate on the surgery one person had to hold Boy's head in position, so that his eye reflections and his breathing could be watched in order that another helper could adjust the many anaesthetic injections for the duration of the operation. Another person was in charge of a solution of saline and glucose and repeatedly injected this intravenously into Boy's tail, to prevent dehydration and shock. To regulate the even dropping of this fluid, the tail had to be secured with a rope to stop Boy twitching it. Then the broken leg was placed in position so that the fractured bones could be stretched with a pulley to face each other. When everything was prepared the vet cut a two and a half inch long slit into the bruised part to locate the fractures. But, without an X-ray photo to guide him to the exact spot, he had to cut off lots of recently grown tissues before he felt the bone through which he could drill holes and insert two thirteen inch long stainless steel pins to join the fractured bones. In the process of removing the superfluous growth Boy lost a lot of blood, which had constantly to be mopped away; as well as this, many retractors and skin-holding forceps which prevented the skin falling back into the open wound, had to be adjusted frequently to enable the vet to have free movement. When at last he could hammer in the two steel pins he found the marrow cavity of the humerus very small and almost solid bone. This greatly complicated the insertion of the pins, and it was only after three hours of intensive surgery that the wound could be filled up with an antibiotic ointment and stitched together.

As if this exhausting ordeal were not enough, the vet now operated on a recent hernia in Boy's belly. George, who only a short while back had undergone a similar operation, watched with special interest, as the vet slit the skin just wide enough to pull the protruding sac, cut it open, twist the superfluous tissues and cut them off; then, neatly stitching the ends up with steel wire, he finally pushed all back into the stomach.

At last we could all relax and have a cup of tea. The vet earned my fullest admiration for his skill in operating on such a complicated fracture under such improvised conditions. Usually he would have had four vets assisting him, but here we all had had to help as best we could.

Soon after, the group broke up and I went to look for the cubs. All our many activities within their area during the last few days had driven them away; we had had difficulty in locating them but at last found them on a lava plateau between the Mulika and Vasorongi rivers, a few miles from where they had guided me to Boy. The ground there was almost barren with hardly any game except two rhinos. I could not think why the cubs liked it here, but they went back and forth across this stony desert with us stumbling after them over hot lava boulders, carrying the heavy meat basket, with no shade beneath which to feed the cubs.

Today we were lucky in finding them at the sand patch which had been the favourite playground of Whity, Mbili and Tatu. At the same thorn tree – on the rough bark of which they had often sharpened their claws – I now saw Tiny doing just the same. What a contrast were these superbly fit cubs to poor Boy. I prayed that they might never have to go through similar calamities to those he and Pippa had experienced. But all I could do now to help during the short time I was allowed to share their lives was to feed them as best I could, and thus give them strong bones and teeth with which to combat all the dangers of their future lives.

Big Boy was now by far the greediest of the cubs and was the least fussy about what he ate, all he was interested in was that there should be plenty of it. He had developed the habit of dropping his meat into the milk – thus preventing both meat and milk from being stolen by Tiny and Somba. Somba now trusted me fully and knew that I always tried to help her, although I kept my distance when she was eating. Tiny still played up to me, rushing close to get any extra titbit, but when I poked little pieces of tripe nearer to his nose with a stick he looked through it as though there was nothing there; he was a real clown.

A few days later the cubs killed a young ostrich, and we found them next to feathers of the bird with their faces still covered in blood and their bellies burstingly full. I was especially glad to know that they were no longer dependent on my feeding them, as the daily heavy rains made moving very difficult. With Ben away, I not only had to search for the cubs and see that there was always meat ready in case they were hungry, but also had to provide George and Boy with everything they needed since George could not leave Boy alone. They were thirty miles from where I had to collect the goats. I sometimes had to make two trips across very slippery roads, often being obliged to dig the Land-Rover out of ditches and, when moving, churning slowly through the mud.

Poor Boy, he had a lot to fill out now and ate and ate, but still was always hungry. It was pathetic to see him hobbling as best he could to meet us at the gate of the fence, staggering and falling down exhausted even by this short distance. The news of his and George's return to camp had quickly gone round and I often found the camp besieged by the lions and their offspring that George had looked after. They were obviously bewildered at seeing Boy so ill and confined inside the fence, from where he looked at his large harem with a sad expression.

Little Sandie was always with the pride and, judging by her bouncy behaviour and good condition, was once more fully accepted by the lions. She seemed to have appointed herself the guardian of the very small cubs of another lioness belonging to the pride, and took her role as 'Aunt' extremely seriously.

It was clear that Boy would not recover enough to live wild again by the date that the Warden had given as an ultimatum, and I therefore suggested to George that he should have a large enclosure erected at our new home on Lake Naivasha, as far away as possible from the main house, so that Boy could recover there without interference. In addition to this, we decided to put up a pre-fab bungalow adjoining the enclosure to enable George to sleep close to Boy and give him as much company as possible. We discussed all this with the Warden, who agreed that Boy could remain in the Park until the end of November when the buildings would be completed.

It rained and rained, and soon most of the park was like a swamp. One morning we found a newly-born drowned buffalo calf carried by the flooded rivulet and lodged against the kitchen bridge. We removed it quickly so as not to attract the crocodiles, which normally kept clear of the camp.

Again we lost Pippa's cubs for several days, but then found them beyond Leopard Rock, fifteen miles from where we had last seen them. Obviously they had been driven away by lions whom we had met on several occasions. We had been given some elephant meat by a hunting party shooting outside the Park, and I now offered this to the cubs. Somba and Tiny turned up their noses, but Big Boy gorged himself on the tough meat until he could hold no more. Two days later I was presented with some buffalo meat which all the cubs liked very much and were at loggerheads over to the last scraps.

Next morning the cubs had moved four miles to the turn-off of the Golo Circuit; close to this was a large acacia which soon became a favourite rendezvous for us. I filmed the cubs eating in star-formation, a typical cheetah habit whereby each animal keeps at an equal distance from the other to get the best elbow space. I was just reloading my camera when a rhino appeared, walking quickly towards us. Instantly all the cubs crouched low, pressed to the ground, but their eyes could still follow the movements of the pachyderm through the grass as it paced towards them. Suddenly it must have got their scent and, swerving round, sniffed the air suspiciously but then it continued towards us. It looked almost as though it was dancing as its round body bobbed along, until again it stopped abruptly. In a flash Somba charged and the rhino crashed away, with her after it. I had been ready with the cine camera to film this ludicrous scene but, unfortunately, a car arrived with visitors, which spoiled any further fun.

The following day we found Somba high up in a tree watching a herd of Grant. After she had made a futile chase she settled to the meat we had brought along, beside her brothers who were already tucking in. Big Boy, as usual, secured the largest part and was still looking round for more although his belly was already like a drum. He was a magnificent animal, much larger now than the other two and extremely handsome but very aloof, and I had the least contact with him.

When at last he had also eaten enough, the cubs chased each other round some doum palm saplings which gave them splendid cover for ambushing each other. How superbly their elegant movements fitted into the group of slender palms outlined against a brilliantly blue sky patterned with Kenya's almost permanent white clouds.

The cubs now remained for some time around Leopard Rock. There were also the six white rhino who, during the night, were kept inside an enclosure, but grazed leisurely around during the daytime with two rangers herding them like cattle.

One morning we fed the cubs and watched them dozing off their meal, when these rhino strolled along. Like lightning the cubs raced away. They must have seen and smelled the tame white rhino many times, and therefore it seemed strange that they now reacted to them as though they were dangerous enemies, while a few days ago they had chased a wild black rhino just for the fun of it. Did they realize that the white rhino were not indigenous here and, for this reason, responded to them as Pippa had done when she once spotted a pair from a great distance?

The roads throughout the Park had deteriorated so badly

during the rains that a tractor had been brought in to try to repair the road to George's camp. But, after ploughing up half the distance, it broke down and the track remained in a knee-deep morass. In my attempts to reach George I often had to balance the Land-Rover along narrow edges of deep ruts, otherwise I sank into the liquid mud and spent hours getting clear. The road to Leopard Rock was not much better and one day I had to wait seven hours before being towed out of the mud. Luckily this happened not far from the cubs so I was able to spend the day with them.

They had found a patch with sandy ground where the rain quickly dried off, and between the showers I could stretch myself near to them. Somba was at first suspicious when our heads were within touching distance, and for a short while she was ready to charge at my slightest move. But when I looked straight into her eyes, without making a sound, she must have sensed my friendly feelings towards her, for she relaxed. Her brothers took no notice of me. The sun burned down on the damp, steamy ground while we all rested, and I listened to the breathing of the cubs and to the chirps of a few sleepy birds – otherwise all was still. How I loved this beautiful Park and all its animals. I had known it now for over twenty-seven years, when George had been in charge of it as Game Warden. Since the time twelve years ago when it became Elsa's home, and later also Pippa's, we had both become even more attached to this area and in a way now regarded it as our spiritual home, though we had of course no legal claim to it.

We had realized from the beginning that our stay here would come to an end once our animals could look after themselves – that indeed had been the object of our experiments. But even though Tiny, Big Boy and Somba had been able to survive without help since the age of fourteen months (compared with Whity, Mbili and Tatu who had had Pippa to take care of them until they were seventeen and a half months old), I wanted to remain with the family until they were of the same age as the previous litter, chiefly to see how their relationship would develop if they started mating.

I had cut short my treatment in London so as to be here during this important phase in their lives – which would be even more interesting to observe since the cubs now had no mother to help them find their territories. It therefore came as a shock to me when I received a letter from the Park Authorities asking me to leave, together with George and Boy, by the end of November. As I had done nothing to justify the shortening of the period which had been agreed upon I wrote to the Park Authorities, and was relieved to get their consent for me to carry on to the end of the year as had been originally arranged.

Meanwhile George tried his best to remove Boy. But the extremely heavy rains made even communication via the radio often difficult, let alone the landing of a plane; not to mention transport by car. George and Boy now shared a small tent. Boy's wound was oozing badly and needed constant treatment. Three times a pilot tried to fly in between the dangerous storms to bring a vet to Meru, only to return to Nairobi defeated, because landing was impossible on the soggy airstrips.

At last he was successful. I had been asked to stand by, when he finally taxied the plane most skilfully between two cloud-bursts on the skiddy ground, so that I could drive the vet instantly to George, while the Warden would follow with the pilot and six rangers shortly afterwards. It was a lucky – though unexpected – coincidence that Ben also arrived with the plane – and we had another hand to help in the difficult task ahead of us. He had been here twice before for brief visits, but now intended to assist me until I left the Park.

Churning along the ten miles to Mugwongo Hill, we took George by surprise. Nevertheless, there was no time to be lost as black cloud-walls threatened more rain. While the vet tranquillized Boy, I packed George's kit into an airbag and helped load his car with the camp equipment. Meanwhile the rest prepared a safe way of lifting Boy into the Land-Rover as soon as he became unconscious.

During all this bustle Girl suddenly arrived. Hopping on to the roof of the Land-Rover outside the fence, which was to carry all the camping kit, she watched as her brother was heaved into a car inside the fence and then driven away for ever from his pride. The Warden took the rest of us, except for Ben who was to cover the rear with the camp kit. But he had not reckoned on Girl. Stubbornly, she remained on the roof of the Land-Rover, and nothing would induce her to leave. It was as if she knew that she was never to see Boy and George again. In the circumstances Ben could do nothing but drive on, with her on top, for about a mile until they saw a herd of giraffe with a young calf. Instantly Girl jumped off, and running after the calf, tipped its leg, making it fall, and then strangled it. When later on Ben described this incident I felt glad that Girl had been distracted by this hunt from watching the departure of her brother, to whom she had not only been devoted all her life but who had also sired two of her litters.

Meanwhile the small four-seater plane had been converted to enable it to carry a 400 pound lion, George, the vet and the pilot. To do this the back seat had been removed and Boy and George were squeezed into its place. All had to be done as quickly as possible, so as to reach Naivasha before dark and avoid a heavy storm which was piling up ahead. I hardly dared look at George. His pale face was drawn while he placed Boy as comfortably as was possible into the small space, then crouched next to him. The vet took the seat near the pilot, who started the engine and took off. The small white plane showed up clearly as it disappeared into the almost black sky. I felt strangely empty all evening.

Although this dramatic departure had been heartbreaking at the time, it turned out to be the best we could have done for Boy under the circumstances. Soon after he had to undergo two more extremely difficult operations, and then had to remain confined at Naivasha for fully nine months.

The rains had once more transformed the dry, straw-coloured plains into luscious pastures with myriads of flowers bursting into bloom every day. Pippa's cubs looked outstandingly beautiful as they walked through fields of sky-blue pentanisia, and I only wished that their mother could have been here to enjoy with me the sight of her lovely children. They were still living within a mile round Leopard Rock, where the ground was comparatively dry and consequently full of game.

Big Boy seemed very attached to Somba lately, both embracing and licking each other most of the time. She had turned into a most handsome female and was by far the greatest character and the most intelligent of the trio; I remembered, filled with guilt, the time when I had thought that she might become a freak. Now she wanted to play with my sandals, and poking at the rubber soles, inched herself close to me. How difficult it was to restrain my wish to respond to her friendly invitation, but I could never forgive myself were I to spoil the cubs now in the last months we were allowed to be together.

12. Love Play among the Cubs

Today was the 1st of December and, in accordance with my agreement with the Warden, I had given the cubs their last meat this morning, filling them up to capacity, after which they dozed close to me with full bellies, as trustingly as ever. Suddenly, baboons barked far away, and in an instant they were off.

The next morning we found them under a bushy tree with branches hanging to the ground. Big Boy was again most affectionate towards Somba who responded in a touching way, embracing him and cuddling close even when he tried to chew at small sticks. Poor Tiny sat apart, or climbed into the tree, as though not interested in what went on between the other two.

After a while they all moved a few hundred yards away to a termite hill, which was completely concealed under a bush. Here Big Boy suddenly uttered a sharp, rattling prr prr – it sounded almost like a cry – and mounted Somba. She squatted as a lioness would while Big Boy rapidly repeated his thrusts for about a minute, after which both relaxed and rested close together, licking and purring.

Tiny had kept as far away as the shade under the bush made it possible. Unfortunately everything happened far too quickly and unexpectedly for me to photograph and adjust the cameras to the dark shade under the bush. After about half-an-hour, the cubs strolled towards the Murera River where they settled under a large tree for the midday lull. I rested close to them, sketching and photographing. But as they slept for most of the time we returned home for a quick lunch. When we came back at teatime the cubs were still drowsy, until a kongoni appeared. Half-heartedly they stalked this large antelope for a short while, then decided against it and sat instead on a large termite hill. The plain round here was like a parkland, covered with small trees and bushes – ideal cheetah country. As soon as it got cooler, the brothers sprayed their 'jets' at a right angle against a few trees. I had often seen them doing this. After first sniffing at a tree, they would turn round and with outstretched tail, squirt liquid in a stream which lasted a second or two against the trunk. Since they repeated these 'jets' two or three times in rapid succession, I assumed that this was how they marked their territory. But never had I seen them 'jetting' with such concentration, and I wondered if they were now warning any rival not to come near Somba. She was obviously aware that she attracted the males, and behaved as seductively as any female would who wanted to arouse a male.

Soon after this the brothers started chasing each other until both landed close to Somba. Tiny now also showed interest in his beguiling sister, but did not quite know what to do; so he mounted Big Boy as well as Somba, and all rolled over in a confused heap.

I was fascinated to watch the coming into puberty of Pippa's children; they were obviously suddenly overwhelmed by this bewildering new urge which, I presumed, for the time being was more of a love play than an actual mating. Unfortunately it soon became too dark for us to see what was happening and we had to return home.

We found the cubs at 8 a.m. the next morning close to the Golo track, within a few hundred yards of the Murera River. It was drizzling, and the trio, full of energy, were having a wild game ambushing each other round the bushes until all tried to climb a fallen tree. Competing for the best position, they often fell off only to repeat the game more vigorously, pulling at each other's tails hoping to drag a rival off the tree. Suddenly, I heard again the sharp, rattling prr prr – and both brothers tried to mate with Somba simultaneously. As this was not possible, Tiny mounted Big Boy while Big Boy mated with Somba. It only lasted for a few minutes but I was luckily in position with the cameras, and hoped I had got some good pictures in spite of the drizzling rain.

As I thought it important to record their first experience of sex, I followed the cubs with notebook and cameras as closely as I could, while asking Local and Stanley to keep at a distance. By now it was 8.15. The cubs rested until 8.30, when the brothers had another chase before mounting each other for a few moments. They repeated this at 8.40, while Somba watched from her bush. She was not as responsive to her amorous brothers today as she had been the day before and, chewing at small sticks, rejected their attempts to mate her; so the poor males, driven by their strange impulse, had to make the best of each other.

At 8.50 Big Boy first ambushed Somba but, since she would not co-operate, he went after Tiny, who quickly struggled up a tree where he was out of reach. After a short while he settled close to Big Boy, both dozing until 9.05 when they again mounted each other. They then went, together with Somba, back to the tree where we had found them on our arrival, which Tiny 'jetted'. Afterwards all had a glorious chase around, racing in the drizzling rain until 9.30 after which they flung themselves panting under bushes for a short rest. When the rain stopped the cubs moved to a termite hill and settled down.

I had noticed previously that the brothers' testicles were always in an upright position in contrast to other mammalian species where they hang down. Today it puzzled me even more to see their erected penes pointing in the opposite direction to the female's vulva, and I could not understand how they could thus mate together; to verify my observations I photographed and sketched the position of their genitals.

The cubs remained quiet until 11.30 when two zebra appeared. Instantly the trio began to stalk. Simultaneously, five vultures appeared and circled close. They must have watched the cubs for some time so as not to lose a moment should there be a kill. But they were in for a disappointment because the cheetah soon gave up the chase and looked for a shady place to rest; Somba went under a bush, and the brothers settled a few yards away on a small termite hill. After scratching a comfortable bed for himself Big Boy ate some grass. Tiny then settled close to him and after a short while both dozed off.

There was no shade for me to rest in from which I could keep a close watch over the trio, except on the same termite hill. But, as this was barely large enough for the brothers, I had to squeeze myself along its base and shift with the moving shade. Luckily the brothers were far too sleepy to mind my being very close to them, and Tiny even pressed his legs alternatively against Big Boy and against me to make sure that he was not alone. He looked so endearing when he was 'all out' that it taxed my principles not to caress him. Big Boy, even in his sleep, was very self-assured, and his relaxed features still expressed all the arrogance of a wild cheetah. Resting so intimately together I almost felt as though I were myself a cheetah.

At about 3 p.m. Somba joined the brothers, who instantly wanted to mate with her. But she was in no responsive mood and so they had to mount each other instead. In spite of its being still rather hot, the cubs then made for the river, Big Boy leading the way. During their short rests Tiny 'jetted' other trees. The banks here were an almost solid wall of the thick undergrowth and, even for cheetah, they were difficult to penetrate. The cubs tried to get through in several places to reach the water but each time retreated, frightened. Somba was particularly nervous and kept well in the rear. At last Big Boy found a spot where all three cubs could reach the water simultaneously.

I had been struggling close behind when, disentangling myself from a net of lianas, I saw the cubs staring intently into a palm-thicket which overhung the river so densely that it was quite impossible to see the opposite bank. Realizing that they were just about to cross over, I hurriedly focused the camera and was in time to photograph Tiny leaping like a streak into the dark brushwood. There followed a splash, and then lots of commotion. Next Big Boy leapt, landed in the fast-running torrent, and scrambled out on to the opposite bank. Finally Somba jumped and she too fell into the water.

There was no point in pursuing the cubs as, by the time we could have reached the other bank, they would have disappeared and spooring would have been impossible in that thick scrub. So we listened to the alarmed shrieks of vervet monkeys who, by the changing direction from which the sound came, gave us a clue as to where the cubs were moving.

Of course I could only blame myself for losing the cubs now; they had obviously had enough of my company and decided that the only way to get rid of me was to cross the river. Normally I would not have been so obtrusive, and my excuse for having followed them so persistently today was to learn all I could about the first sexual reactions of cheetah which, to my knowledge, had never before been observed under natural conditions, let alone photographed.

Hoping to meet up again with the trio we drove a few miles upstream to where we could ford the river in the car. But, as soon as we came on to the plain beyond the riverbush, we ran into so many buffalo that we had to give up, and as it was we reached camp only just before dark.

There we found Ben. He had been away to take some of George's belongings to Naivasha and had extended the trip. I asked him why he had been here very little since my return from London, and in answer he explained he did not like sharing the cheetah with me and preferred being on his own. This was understandable, but not compatible with his being my assistant! Next day he accompanied us in the search for the cubs but kept as much as possible to himself.

The Murera River is the boundary of the Park and the country beyond was new ground for us. It was ideal for cheetah once the extremely thick riverbush, which stretched for about a mile wide around, was left behind. The cause for this extensive belt of vegetation is a most attractive lugga which runs through it and peters out after a few miles; after which the riverbush is again limited to the Murera. Although this lugga only carries running water during the rains a few pools remain during the dry season and attract many animals, probably because here they are not endangered by the crocodiles which infested the Murera. Now, while the rains had not ceased, the thick scrub was in full bloom, and with flowers everywhere in such profusion I found it difficult not to botanize and to make myself concentrate on tracking – which was anyway almost impossible in these conditions.

Gradually the bush opened into beautiful parkland, dotted with many termite hills which offered splendid look-outs, and groups of bushy trees under which a predator could wait, concealed and comfortably cool in the shade, for prey to pass by. In short it would have been an ideal hunting-ground for Pippa's cubs, had it been protected. But it belonged to the Boran tribesmen who refused to sell the 300 square miles of wooden plain to the National Parks, even though it was infested with tsetse fly and useless for livestock. However it was much frequented by poachers; luckily they concentrated along the Bisanadi River, which was the only water supply for animals in the area beyond the Murera. Since the Bisanadi was a good distance away we hoped that Pippa's cubs would keep to the Murera, but, in spite of making a thorough search along its banks, we had no luck in finding them.

Next morning I asked Ben to collect the wire fence from George's camp, and on our return that evening, from yet one more futile search, I found a note from him to say that he had again injured his leg and had driven to the hospital in Nairobi. He never returned.

We now concentrated our searches on the Boran country. Day after day we crossed and re-crossed the flooded Murera, looking for fresh tracks on its banks before walking for miles on the plains beyond. That we got drenched by cloud-bursts was of no importance as long as I could keep the cameras dry. On one occasion three elephants left us no choice but to wade through the river at a place where two large crocodiles slithered into the water at our approach. By throwing stones and splashing a lot, we safely reached the farther bank, but I became more than ever concerned about the cubs.

After five days we found the remains of a gerenuk gazelle near Leopard Rock with cheetah spoor around it. And after two more days again saw fresh cheetah spoor close to the rhino paddocks. Not far from here some vultures guided us to a dead giraffe – a lion was sitting close to the carcass. As soon as he saw us, he made off and thus gave us an opportunity to investigate the kill, but when we reached the scene, we found the giraffe's body untouched except for the eyes and tongue where the vultures had already done their gruesome job. Only the head, neck and back were visible, the rest having been sucked in by liquid mud and completely submerged. Judging by the swampy surroundings, the poor giraffe must have got bogged down when crossing over the morass, and died a horrible, lingering death. I could only hope that the vultures arrived later. Local managed to cut off the end of its tail to hand later to the Warden as evidence of a natural death.

13. Last Days with the Cubs

Meanwhile seven precious days of my last month with the cheetah had passed without our finding the cubs. As we were driving home late one afternoon, following a sudden impulse we turned off the main road on to the Golo track, although it meant driving straight into a storm. We had not gone a hundred yards when we spotted the cubs racing towards us; just then the sun broke through the pitch black sky and for a few moments lit up their light elegant bodies in striking contrast to the dramatic background. They were in excellent condition and had obviously killed the gerenuk whose bones we had found not far from here. All the same the cubs were hungry, but I had nothing to offer them, so I quickly took a few photographs before the first big drops fell and drenched the cubs. Huddling close together and shaking the water off their coats, they soon got disgusted and walked off to a bush for shelter. When I attempted to turn the car round, we got thoroughly bogged down. While digging ourselves out it was our turn to get drenched, then we drove home at a funereal pace through foot-deep ruts filled with running water.

For the next two days we searched in vain except that we found the pugmarks of the cubs, from which we learned that they had chased a young buffalo on their way to the lava plateau. Concentrating on this area, I had to take my megaphone along to save my voice which was already hoarse from calling 'Pippa, Pippa, Pippa' all day long. Tiny was the first to respond; soon after Big Boy appeared and, finally, Somba followed; all panting heavily. They must have been hunting although we had only seen a rhino here, one we knew from our previous searches across this stony place. The cubs were very hungry and had evidently not killed for at least three

...ove play would start gently with clasping

...or with a mock fight

'Jetting'

Mating

...and the final neck bite

Resting under a bush

Often all three cubs would flirt

…and mate

Love play would continue

Licking noses

....licking tongues

An ambush

Mating

days. Trustfully, they sat around us, waiting for the meat which I was no longer allowed to give them.

It was already hot and the cubs settled under a small bush with hardly enough shade to keep them cool. They dozed off with their feet across each other to keep physical contact, but at 2 p.m. became restless and moved on. I could judge how hungry they were by the fact that when they realized that I had no meat for them they hunted during the hottest time of the day. I screened the surroundings with my field-glasses, but when I saw nothing for them to kill I walked in the direction of Leopard Rock where there was more game, hoping that they would follow.

They did. It was a long, hot walk and they rested when-ever they could find some meagre shade. Tiny was very tired and hungry; he always purred whenever I came near and made me wretched, knowing that I would have nothing to offer them in the end, except perhaps to lead them to a kill. While the brothers dragged themselves along Somba was con-stantly searching for anything moving, but we only met three elephants before reaching the main road near the Golo turn-off where I had left the Land-Rover. Hoping to get some-thing to eat at last, the cubs sniffed round the car, but as there was nothing forthcoming they settled on a nearby termite hill from where they looked at me with such reproachful expres-sions that I felt miserable. Somba especially seemed to be saying 'Why did you lead us such a long way only to let us down?'

Then I spotted two Grant's gazelles a long way off. I tried to round them up and chase them towards the cubs but was defeated by a buffalo, who suddenly emerged from a bush and walked in between the Grants and me. Then Local and Stan-ley tried their luck while I drew the cubs' attention to the gazelles which they had not yet spotted. But at that moment, more buffalo appeared and spoiled our teamwork. As it was rapidly getting darker I could do nothing but drive quickly away – hoping that the cubs would stay on and find the

Grants. All that day I had seen no sign of the cubs mating, except that Somba had kept close to Big Boy.

The following morning the cubs came rushing from the plain towards the car and settled on the same termite hill where we had left them the evening before. They had not killed in spite of there being eight Grants in view. Again I tried my best to guide the cubs to them, but they just moved to the next shady tree to sleep. Later on they walked to a small hill, where it was too sunny for me to sketch; so I wrote letters inside the car while they had their midday nap. At 2 p.m. they again moved on, this time towards the Murera which was about a mile off. Somba led the way. Listening alertly to the faintest sound, she moved slowly step by step with outstretched neck, often keeping a front leg suspended to avoid the slightest noise, and circling every thicket in which a small antelope might hide. Sometimes she was helped by Tiny who circled the opposite side of the bush. Her face was beautiful as she hunted; she seemed so happy and reminded me very much of Pippa. It was strange that all three of these cubs had a far more rounded tip to their noses than Pippa or any of her previous litters had had.

At last Somba and Big Boy stirred up a Lesser Kudu male and gave it a good chase. I was surprised that they should be interested in such a large buck and was much relieved when they soon gave up the hunt. Farther on we saw a few eland, oryx and giraffe, but all of these were much too big for cheetah to tackle.

Having now been on the move without a rest for three hours, the cubs retreated to a bush. Here they were close to the river, and being afraid that they might cross it again if I pursued them too persistently, I withdrew although it was only teatime. At sunset the Warden saw them at Leopard Rock. That was the last we knew of their whereabouts for the next few days.

Tracking from dawn to dusk, one late afternoon we followed some fifty vultures which we saw descending on a tree. We hoped that they would lead us to the cubs on a kill. At our approach, all flew off to another tree and repeated this performance whenever we came near. There was no trace of a carcass, nor any spoor of predators which might have accounted for such a large congregation of various species of birds of prey.

Another time we settled for lunch at the Murera after an exasperating search which had lasted all morning. The river here rushed past a rocky cliff, thickly overgrown with palms, figs and acacias, all linked together by creepers to form a green dome under whose shade we picnicked. Although the river below made a roaring noise, and insects and birds enlivened the place wherever I looked, there was an eeriness around, a timelessness which was as permanent as life and which one sensed would continue to exist as long as life itself. Why was it that here I felt 'safe', while in the civilized world man has invented round himself I never felt secure? Was it because we try to interfere with and to control life, which is essentially uncontrollable? Animals, living for the moment and adapting themselves to the unforeseen, have survived for millions of years; if we try to control everything can we too survive? Here there was a permanence which involved every form of life but in the civilized places there is only man. If only, I thought, I could help preserve this permanence by first helping the wild animals to survive. Since they are the key to our understanding of the 'whole', if I could do this I felt that my life would not have been wasted. I was now closer than ever to probing into the hitherto unknown facts of the lives of cheetah; for instance, how they react to puberty – but it was going to be denied to me to lift more of this veil because of the restrictions to which I must submit.

It was now the 15th of December – only a few more days left in which to share the cheetah's lives, and it was distressing that so many of these were being wasted in searching for the cubs. My hunch told me that they were still in Boran country, and there we found them the following day. They had still not killed, and now, after seven days of fasting, their pelvic bones stuck out alarmingly. They had tried hard to hunt, but the grass was now very high and this made it difficult for them to find a kill. I decided to feed them. I felt more than justified as I did not want them to lose condition while they were mating, nor did I want to lose touch with them and miss a unique opportunity to learn more about their sexual behaviour. Also I told myself that they were now outside the Park's boundary, and therefore beyond the jurisdiction of the authorities.

While I collected a goat, I left Local behind to watch the cubs' movements. On my return he told me that Somba had mock-charged him whenever he moved, but had not objected to his presence as long as he stood still. They jumped ravenously at the carcass and finished it within half-an-hour. After making sure that nothing edible had been left, they moved to a tree. I followed as usual with my sketchbook but, by moving to another tree, the cubs made it plain that I was not welcome. After a little while I again tried my luck, with the same result. So I watched them from a safe distance through my binoculars, and noticed that whenever Tiny licked and embraced Big Boy his penis protruded, though he always kept apart when Big Boy flirted with Somba.

Next morning we found the cubs at the same lugga, which farther downstream traversed the Murera's wide belt of vegetation, but here ran through an open plain with a few isolated doum palms and suaki bushes growing along its banks. They provided perfect shelter for the cheetah during the hot hours of the day, as well as a good look-out over the surroundings. The water was only a few inches deep and would have been an ideal playground, but the cubs never wetted their feet more than necessary and preferred jumping across it. Their bellies were still round from yesterday's feast, so I did not feed them again and only watched them playing and licking each other. They obviously resented my presence and moved away whenever I came near, so we returned home at 2 p.m.

The following morning thick fog reduced visibility to a few yards. I parked the car under a terminalia from where we would have had a splendid view across the plain and lugga under normal weather conditions, but today I had to rely on my hooting signal to attract the cheetah. It only took a short time before three very hungry cubs emerged from out of the mist. They were covered with ticks. Never before had I seen them so badly plagued by these parasites, but my attempts to pull some off were not appreciated and so I left to fetch a goat to fill their empty stomachs.

Meanwhile the weather cleared up and, on my return, the sun was already burning so fiercely that I fed the cubs right under the terminalia which provided shade for all of us. Big Boy gobbled his meat twice as fast as Tiny, who slowly and contentedly chewed the fatty tissues lining the goatskin. He was so fond of this that he ignored the more substantial food which I saved for him from his greedy brother and sister. To-day the cubs showed no sexual impulses, but again moved away from me once they had finished eating.

The next day we found them still near the terminalia, which became from now on our rendezvous. I watched them cuddling up together, hugging each other in a way which I could only interpret as 'love play'. After about two hours, Tiny became very 'sexy' and, snuggling up to Big Boy, clasped him affectionately, while both their penes protruded. Finally they ran off to the nearest tree, sniffed around it and – with rigid tail – 'jetted' it. After having repeated this several times, they chased each other round in circles, then, standing on their hind legs, spanked each other, becoming more and more excited until – prr prr – they mounted each other, trying to copulate.

Somba calmly watched her brothers and as soon as their mating attempts ended, she ambled off to the lugga. Instantly, Tiny and Big Boy followed her and all disappeared inside a suaki bush where they found a perfect lair right on the edge of the running water. I could only get glimpses of the cubs through the densely-wooded bush, but even so they looked at me as if to say, at last we have found a place where you can't follow us.

Next morning, the 19th of December, a thick mist once again enshrouded the Park. We had followed the cubs' spoor for over three hours and once more I had called 'Pippa, Pippa, Pippa'; finally I saw a cheetah sitting in a tree. I watched it for some time, but nothing happened. I called again, but still this cheetah did not respond. I was puzzled. If it was one of the trio why did the others not turn up, but if this cheetah was wild, why did it not bolt? Leaving the men behind, I walked slowly towards it, until I suddenly recognized Whity. She had obviously heard the familiar Pippa call and come along. She was in perfect health, very large, and still had the same charm she had had when she was a cub.

In case of an emergency we always carried a tin of evaporated milk, which I now offered Whity. Although it was two years and three months since I had last fed her, and I had only seen her once a year ago when she was highly pregnant, she now came just as trustingly as if we had never parted and drank the milk within a few feet of me. Then she moved to a fallen tree and, sitting on it silhouetted against the sky, posed superbly for photographs. I offered her more milk, holding the bowl right up to her, to which she responded with a little growl but nevertheless lapped the bowl clean. Finally she surveyed the bush most carefully, hopped off the tree, and vanished back into her world. Watching her disappear slowly, I felt extremely happy. Whity had been living completely wild for more than two years now. Remembering her previous pregnancy, I thought she might even at this very moment be returning to her cubs, and yet she still accepted me as her old friend but without showing any wish to follow us back to her former home. If I could think of a reward for all the heartbreaks I had undergone during the last years, this truly was the greatest one I could have asked for.

A short while afterwards we met our trio about half a mile away. I wondered if they had already met up with Whity, and if so how they had reacted to each other. Would Whity 'mother' them, or treat them as intruders upon her territory? Or might she be attracted to Big Boy and Tiny, and fight Somba as a rival? Today the cubs did not seem inclined to mate, but as they were very hungry I left Local in charge of them and went off to fetch a goat.

During the two hours I was away he managed to lead the cubs to the terminalia, where I found the party waiting on my return. In no time the carcass was eaten up, and the cubs retreated for a rest. Soon they were too sleepy to resent my presence and I could sit with them, photographing and sketching. I found it very frustrating adhering to my rule of not touching them, particularly when Somba's silky tail brushed against my legs. But thinking of Whity reminded me that I must never be possessive in my love for these cubs if I wanted them to live as happy and wild as Pippa's previous litter was now living.

The following morning we searched again until midday, only to find the cubs waiting at the terminalia tree where I had left the car. All were in a playful mood, especially Tiny. Overcome by sexual desire, he challenged not only Somba and Big Boy, but rolled against trees and rushed wildly around as if he did not know how to appease this overpowering urge. At last he settled, quite exhausted, near Somba and Big Boy, and all three dozed off.

I knew the cubs would now rest during the hot hours, so I could safely drive away to find out how close the nearest Boran settlements were from here. I was worried as I had heard of a new scheme for encouraging the Boran to plant crops near this area. Driving along the boundary road I had to pass through densely-wooded forest for about a mile. Knowing the cubs' preference for open ground I hoped this might deter them from exploring the country beyond.

Then I had to ford the Bisanadi and, after another two miles across open plain, reached the Kinna River which here runs parallel to the Bisanadi before flowing into it a few miles downstream. As soon as I had crossed the Kinna I saw the first flimsy grass-huts of the Boran, with patches of rice and maize around, and a few skinny goats browsing – we were barely four miles from where the cubs were now resting. My only hope now was that the cubs would find the country in the opposite direction more attractive, and would rely on their instincts to keep clear of strangers.

On my return, at teatime, they came rushing up to the car expecting a meal, but when they found no goat they started to play, rolling together and licking and embracing each other very gently for about an hour. Both males then went over to the nearest tree to 'jet' it. After ambushing and knocking each other over, they played the spanking game until – prr prr – all three mated in wild confusion. I now noticed for the first time that the males nibbled Somba's neck when they had concluded mating, exactly as the lion does to the lioness. But though the cubs obeyed an innate impulse, the brothers bit too hard and pulled poor Somba's skin so high that she cried out and cuffed them. In consequence the brothers now mounted each other, but without the final neck bite. As on previous occasions when the cubs had been overcome by sexual impetus, they resented my presence and moved across the lugga. So as not to chase them farther into Boran country I withdrew.

For the next four days I did not see the cubs mating, although they may have done so in the early mornings when we were still searching for them. They were most affectionate and gentle with each other at all times, and even during the hot hours kept in intimate contact, holding one another close and often licking each other's tongues. The brothers frequently 'jetted' trees, sometimes the same tree but not at the same time. Somba never indulged in such 'markings', though she often defecated on a tree-stump or a termite hill if one were near at the time.

During these days the cubs remained within a mile of the terminalia, though we sometimes had to search for several hours before finding them. On two successive days the trio watched a herd of Grant with great interest, but seemed only to have succeeded in making a kill on the third day, when we found them with bulging bellies. Unknowingly, they had helped themselves to their Christmas dinner.

It was now the fifth Christmas since I had camped with Pippa and her cubs in Meru Park, and sadly it was to be our last here. As if to console us for Pippa's absence the whole countryside had transformed itself into a fantastic Christmas stage set. Early in the morning the bush had been heavy with dew and every drop was sparkling in all the colours of the spectrum; in particular the spider-webs glistened against the sun like scintillating Christmas decorations, embellishing each branch until later on the hot sun extinguished this glittering phenomenon.

On Christmas morning the cubs again rejoiced in an intensive love play with a final mating. Up to now they had always followed a routine, caressing each other for at least half-an-hour, the males then 'jetting' the trees, after which they chased round in vigorous play together with the female, until the sharp, rattling prr prr preceded their mating which only lasted a few minutes. They then rested during the hot hours and sometimes allowed me to sit close by. Today I was so privileged, even Somba no longer felt suspicious and sometimes pressed her legs against mine. Tiny was the least inclined for such familiarities, though he knew he was my favourite. He was still rather frail compared with Big Boy, but always active and touching.

At teatime the cubs strolled to the lugga and had a glorious game: Tiny paraded a doum palm leaf provokingly and was promptly chased by the others, all rolling over each other until they forgot about the leaf and jumped back and forth across the lugga. By doing this they upset all the frogs in the vicinity, who plopped into the water like pennies into a wishing fountain. Intrigued, the cubs now settled on the bank and watched the frogs until it got dark and we had to go home.

Next morning we found them hunting. I followed at a distance so as not to interfere but from which I could observe they were looking into every thicket and listening for the faintest sound. But nothing stirred except a buffalo, who rose sleepily from the grass and, luckily for me, ambled off in the opposite direction. Soon after I saw the brothers clambering up a termite hill, but jumping down instantly and bolting as fast as they could. I then spotted a troop of baboons a long way off, popping up and down in the high grass. Although the cubs were almost fully grown they still dreaded baboons because of the advantage they possessed by being able to shin up the smooth stems of doum palms, which a cheetah could not do.

Later on we detected Tiny high up in an acacia tree, looking for a kill. At my approach he started purring, asking for food. The cubs were evidently very hungry and, as I could not see any game around except for a few giraffe, I collected a goat. Knowing that wild cheetah kill, on average, every second day I had followed this routine when feeding the cubs if they were unable to find a prey. Later, watching them devour the goat, I was amused to see Tiny and Somba at loggerheads over a piece of meat, completely ignoring the fact that Big Boy was meanwhile gobbling up most of the remaining carcass. While Tiny was engrossed in his contest with Somba he uttered a new squealing sound which seemed to intimidate his sister; then he relaxed and started to eat. Within a few seconds both cubs were chewing amicably at the same piece of meat, each facing the other. When finally the cubs had licked up the last scrap, they moved to the lugga and disappeared into a thicket for the rest of the day.

On the following morning, the 29th of December, we

found them intently watching a gerenuk. Somba crept low on the ground towards the gazelle, only to stir up two buffalo which upset her stalk. So the cubs moved slowly to the lugga, where Tiny suddenly seemed to be overcome by a violent sexual urge, so strong that he almost attacked Big Boy. Meanwhile the buffaloes had caught up, and holding up their massive heads, sniffing our scent, remained not more than a hundred yards away. Their presence did not deter Tiny from persistently following Big Boy until he mounted him, close to the lugga where the bank fell away in a steep wall some five yards deep. The two were so absorbed in their sexual excitement that they did not notice they were getting nearer and nearer to the edge, until both suddenly landed with a splash in the water below. I could not help laughing aloud, but regretted doing so for I have never seen two cheetah more embarrassed than the brothers were as they shook themselves dry and waded very subdued on to dry ground. Of course that was the end of Tiny's amorous desire. To give them time to recover their dignity I retreated to the car to write letters, while they went off for their midday slumber to a shady bush not far away.

By teatime Tiny again became restless, and I was just in time to film the brothers mounting each other. Both seemed quite oblivious of my presence and copulated at my very feet, while Somba rested within touching distance of me, watching all this calmly.

As soon as the brothers relaxed, Big Boy moved off. It was still very hot; nevertheless, he walked resolutely on so that Tiny and Somba had no choice other than to follow if they did not wish to be left behind. Despite the fact that I had given them a goat only the day before, all seemed extremely hungry and were now obviously on the hunt. Although Big Boy was the leader he left the hard work to Somba, who never missed a tree from which she could look around and was by far the most alert. Tiny was normally also a very active hunter, but he was suffering from the heat and only reluctantly played his part.

After we had walked for about an hour the cubs, panting heavily, flung themselves under a shady bush, each separated by a few yards, while I settled myself within touching distance of Tiny. He was a picture of beauty as he rose out of the waving grass, silhouetted against a deep blue sky intensified by the late afternoon sun. But for me he was far more than a perfect wild animal in the grandeur of the African plain. For me, it was as if we had been switched back to the time when man and beast were still united in harmony and trusted each other. How I longed to put my arms around Tiny – to hold this moment for ever. But I knew that in a few days' time the spell would have to be broken and that I had to prepare Tiny for a future in which his trust in other humans should never bring him to harm. Meanwhile I dragged out these minutes, only too painfully aware that in a short while all this would be no more than a precious memory.

Luckily the cubs, spared my anguish, soon pursued their hunt. Moving much farther into Boran country than I had known them go before, they at last spotted a few zebra with a foal. Big Boy and Somba quickly climbed a tree and Tiny struggled up into a forked branch from where all watched the herd intently. Contemplating the hunt for a very long time, they finally decided against it and settled under a tree. I was much relieved as the foal was already too big for the cubs to tackle.

I looked at the trio. They were so beautiful as they rested in the warm glow of the setting sun. I thought of Pippa, and only hoped that the cubs did not miss her as much as I did. By now the light was fading fast and we had to hurry home.

When we arrived at the terminalia early next morning, I detected through my field-glasses two lions walking along the lugga and disappearing in the direction where we had left the cubs. Although I feared that the cheetah, hearing these lions, might have cleared out we retraced step by step the ground where we had last seen them, but could find no trace of the family.

Next day we walked eight hours in exhausting heat through perfect cheetah country, criss-crossed with duiker spoor, but again found no sign of our cubs. The following day we explored new ground from dawn to dusk, including a large forest belt leading towards the Bisanadi River where the undergrowth was so thick that Local had repeatedly to climb up trees to find our bearings. This was the last day we were allowed to be together with the cubs and I was desperate to find them. Of course my reasoning told me that it was much better for them to have deserted us while they were intent on a hunt, than if they had relied on my feeding them up to the last moment and then found themselves abandoned when, against my will, I had to withdraw for good. Nevertheless, it was hard to leave here now without having seen the cubs once more.

At least I could console myself that Pippa's children were all now able to live completely wild, and that I had left them in the best possible condition to cope with whatever was in store for them. Naturally I would have liked to have carried on for as long as it would take to learn if Somba, at the age of seventeen months, had already conceived; and if the brothers would help to feed her before and after she gave birth; and to know when the trio would split up, and how they would then distribute their territories; into what areas they would extend them not to infringe on Pippa's former litter, and how they would react to each other.

But although I explained to the Park Authorities the unique opportunities I still had to learn about the unknown habits of cheetah, all my appeals for an extension to my stay here were turned down. So there was nothing more for me to do but to visit the Park periodically in the future and hope to contact Pippa's cubs again. The Warden agreed to my camping on these occasions on our camp-site and said he would allow Local to help me search if I paid him a salary additional to his wages as Chief White Rhino Ranger, to which he had now been appointed. Finally, the Warden offered to waive the entrance fees whenever I wanted to visit Meru, and thus we parted on the 2nd of January 1970.

14. Frustrating Visits to Meru Park

I was not able to return before the 25th of March because of a third operation on my hand which took a long time to heal.

By then, the short but heavy rains were due again. Ignoring the bad weather forecast I drove, with Stanley, the day-long trip to Meru. Of course I knew that my camp had been burnt down when we had left the Park in January; nevertheless, it was a shock when we arrived, late in the afternoon, to see what had been my home for four and a half years completely demolished, and the ground covered with ashes. Stanley and Local were overjoyed to see each other again, and I was grateful for their cheerful chatter which broke the sad stillness all around.

After we had pitched our tents they retired to their quarters, and I went to Pippa's grave. This was the only thing now left from our once happy home, and was the guardian of my memories. At dawn I woke to the sleepy twitter of a bird. Here, no walls divided us as in the comfortable house at Lake Naivasha, and I could be a part of all these merry birds who were now heralding the rising sun.

As soon as Stanley brought the morning tea, all my old friends turned up expecting their usual breakfast too. The waxbills, weavers and pigeons waiting for their millet, and the superb starlings for their bacon rinds; even the odd, deformed young starling came – he had been at the very bottom of the 'pecking hierarchy' when he was tiny, but now made up for it by hopping right inside the tent and almost nudging my feet. I had brought enough food not to disappoint the birds, though I had not expected such unchanging trust from all my friends.

I then made a quick inspection of everything around the

camp. The few patches of coarse grass that had been near the camp had now spread all around and, since no burning had been done here for two years, such a jungle had grown up that only elephants, giraffe or buffalo could browse here unconcerned about predators. I could well understand why none of Pippa's children had returned to this spot since her death. Unless burning were soon resumed the area would turn into a woody scrub, useless for any smaller animals.

Seeing heavy rain-clouds piling up all round, I knew there was no time to lose if I were to find the cubs today. On our drive we spotted a full-grown giraffe whose neck after turning, about halfway up its length, at a sharp right angle, continued in a horizontal direction for about a foot and then turned equally abruptly into a vertical position again. Despite this extraordinary kink, the giraffe seemed neither handicapped in browsing, nor in her movements, and was obviously accepted by the herd.

Unfortunately that was the only memorable thing we saw during the next three days, during which we very often got drenched and we spent most of our time digging the Land-Rover free of mud. Since spooring had become impossible on the soaked ground, I decided to return to Naivasha before we might find ourselves marooned for weeks. I left with a heavy heart, having achieved nothing except to learn that the cubs had last been seen in January near the border road close to the Bisanadi.

My second trip between the 20th and the 26th of July was more rewarding. On our arrival I was told that recently a friendly female cheetah with a three month old cub had been seen for several days near the Hans Lugga together with a very nervous male. It was assumed that she was one of Pippa's daughters. Further two large males had been seen close to the Murera Gate, they were believed to be Tiny and Big Boy. Another female with two cubs had frequently been observed near Kenmare Lodge; she too had behaved like one of Pippa's daughters, and besides this, a female and two cubs had been reported across the Rojoweru, as well as a single male near the White Rhino *boma*. Though all these reports sounded very promising, I was only going to believe them after myself identifying Pippa's children by their tail-root spots.

Already on the first day we were lucky. As we drove in the early morning along the track near the Mulika swamp, some vultures attracted our attention and then I noticed a cheetah sitting under a bush about a hundred yards off the track. It remained in the same position when I walked slowly towards it calling 'Pippa'. After I had come within twenty yards of it, two almost fully grown cubs broke cover and bolted, while the mother looked straight into my eyes and only moved away when I came within touching distance. The moment I saw her hindquarters I identified her as Tatu. It was two years and ten months since I had last fed her, and I had not seen her for a year and seven months, and then only for a few moments. Judging by the size of her cubs she must have then been pregnant, just when Whity was.

After a short run Tatu stopped, and let me approach her with a bowl of milk. I placed it on the ground, but she ignored it and moved on; she had always been extremely fond of milk and so I tried again, but she refused even to look at it and walked away whenever I showed her the bowl. Thus we continued in the direction in which her cubs had disappeared, with Local following at a safe distance. Tatu called frequently in the low moan which I knew so well because Pippa had used it when she was worried about her cubs. Finally Tatu sat down and I settled nearby under a tree. We were within a few hundred yards of the Mulika and not far from the place which, soon after I had brought her to the Park, Pippa had for three months chosen as her headquarters. It was wonderful to be here now with Pippa's daughter and her grandchildren, who were of roughly the same age as Pippa had then been.

When Tatu had stopped calling, she still kept on looking

intently towards the Mulika. Assuming that her cubs were frightened by my presence, and that she did not want to give away their whereabouts, we returned to camp at 2 p.m. for a quick lunch. When we came back at teatime I caught a glimpse of the two cubs running fast to the rivulet, but they were too far away for me to ascertain their age. Tatu was still in the same spot where I had left her, preoccupied with licking her groin. After she had relaxed I could see that she had been licking an open wound the size of my hand; the skin around was black, but otherwise the wound looked clean. I was horrified. I had not noticed any limp or stiffness during the morning. I could not imagine what could have caused such a ghastly wound for the place was far too protected to have been torn during a fight and the exposed flesh did not seem to be damaged. The only explanation I could think of was either a tick-bite, which could start up an abscess that might destroy the tissues, or a snakebite which had only just penetrated the skin but had an equally damaging effect on the surroundings. I tried to get a better view of the wound and even a photograph to show the vet, but Tatu did not allow me to come close enough for either and walked on, calling the cubs constantly, until she reached the rivulet. Here she gazed across the water where no doubt her cubs were hiding. Following the direction of her eyes, I only saw a rhino moving steadily towards us. Tatu looked so splendid, as she stood on a termite hill in the setting sun, that nobody would have suspected she was suffering from such a terrible wound. I did not want her to cross the Mulika, so decided to go home and ask the Warden for help.

After having explained the case to him, he agreed that I could feed Tatu to speed up her recovery. So early next morning we went to get a goat, but spent the best part of the day before we found one for sale right in the Boran country. When we arrived with it in the late afternoon at the place where I had left Tatu, we learned from her spoor that she had crossed the Mulika and joined her cubs, but had then covered such rocky ground that we lost all trace of them. From now on we concentrated on finding Tatu, but day after day passed in exhausting searches without our seeing a trace of her and her cubs. Nor did we find any of the fourteen cheetah that had been seen during the previous week, though we could verify their presence by their spoor.

As far as I could judge the age of Tatu's cubs they might just have been able, but only just, to have assisted her, after her injury, in hunting – and indeed if not how could all three have survived? Driven to panic by the thought that Tatu might further injure herself by hunting, we covered an enormous amount of ground on foot and by car, but the grass was now so high everywhere that we could easily have passed within a few feet of a cheetah without seeing it if it did not wish to be seen. Knowing what masters they are at hiding themselves, our searches seemed pretty hopeless.

As I had booked in for yet a fourth operation on my hand, which was to take place in a few days' time, we left the Park but decided to return early in October, when the burning of the grass before the rains would make it easier to see the cubs on the black ground.

My third visit to Meru was to last from the 5th to the 23rd of October. On our first morning at Pippa's camp the birds were just as friendly as they had ever been and queued up for their titbits. Equally conservative were the two Grant's gazelles and five Grevy's zebra which we found later on our drive still grazing the same territory which they had occupied during the five years I had known them. This was also true of my old friend, the hammerkop, who had always fished at the limestone crossing downstream near the camp, and was still using his old home although he now had a concrete ford to fish from; I was glad he had survived the extensive roadworks all around which had recently opened up the plains to visitors.

I was acutely aware of how lucky I had been living here

with Pippa while most of the Park was still untouched. Although the Elsa Wild Animal Appeal had provided funds to help with its development, it nevertheless gave me a pang to see so many new highways cutting straight lines through Pippa's world.

A little later, when passing the Mulika sand patch which had been one of Pippa's favourite playgrounds, I noticed two ears twitching above the grass some distance away. Hoping that they might belong to one of Pippa's cubs, I called her name, only to stir up a young lioness who slunk off when we approached.

Half a mile farther on we followed many vultures descending on to the ridge, where they landed on a heap of marabou storks who were attacking the dried-up carcass of an elephant. The tusks had been removed but otherwise the elephant was complete and looked like a mummy. It must have died a considerable time ago and I could not imagine what food these scavenging birds could find under the taut, thick skin stretched across the bare skeleton.

We spent the rest of the day in a fruitless search for the cubs, and returned in the late afternoon to the camp. It was the 7th of October, and the first anniversary of Pippa's death. On our previous visit I had noticed a few cracks in her grave, possibly made by baboons. Judging by their droppings on the cairn they seemed to use it as a playground, and may well have scratched at the cement joints in search of the lizards and beetles which always sunned themselves on the slabs. I had brought cement along, so now I filled in the fissures and repaired the damage.

Afterwards I sat with my back against the grave as I had often done before. The moon had risen and filled the bush around with a silvery haze which softened its contrasts. All was so peaceful here. If only I could have my mind set at rest about the fate of Pippa's cubs. It did not help to tell myself that even Pippa, who had always been very concerned about her children while they were still dependent on her help, had, once they could look after themselves, painlessly abandoned them. Although I knew that this was part of nature's law it did not give me the certainty that all was well with them. So we continued our search early next morning, and carried on day after day, driving for many hours to reach the areas at the extreme ends of the Park where we suspected Pippa's cubs to be.

Once, near George's former camp, we saw a cheetah in the far distance but, when I called Pippa's name and started walking towards it, it vanished. We then observed many vultures flying to the far end of the extensive swamp which surrounded his old camp. It took me about half-an-hour before I managed to drive the Land-Rover over the extremely rough ground near enough to see a young lioness walking steadily towards the spot which had attracted the birds, who flew off to the nearest tree at her approach. As soon as she had reached the place a rhino got up and faced her; both stood still. After a while the lioness prodded the rhino's nose; this it resented and stepped back a few feet. There it remained facing the lioness who after a few minutes sat down without taking her eyes off the rhino. Then the rhino turned and slowly walked a few yards away. Instantly the lioness picked up a carcass which had been lying between them, but which had been hidden from us by the grass. From our position, some 400 yards away, neither of us could make out what kind of carcass she now straddled, but it must have been a heavy load for it took her a long time to drag it out of sight. Normally lion and rhino avoid each other, and in this case the rhino must have had an interest in the carcass to stand its ground for so long. I could only assume that the rhino had had a miscarriage, which had been spotted by the vultures who had guided the lioness and ourselves to the 'kill'; it had taken both of us some time before we arrived simultaneously on the scene. The rhino that had defended the dead calf had by now walked away, something it would certainly not have done had the calf been alive.

We had intended having a picnic lunch at George's old camp-site but found it occupied by a herd of impala. It was a beautiful sight to watch these graceful antelopes standing between the two trees that had previously overshadowed George's camp. The impala looked more like a frieze than living animals as they stood absolutely still in the shade waiting for the midday heat to abate. The ground around was already completely overgrown and one could hardly believe that barely a year ago this place had been teeming with human activity. It seemed ironical that nature had so quickly reclaimed the land from man's interferences, while all around new circuits cut like fresh wounds into the pristine plains. Along these we often found the spoor of cheetah, who used the roads as highways. But, even if we tracked them like bloodhounds for many miles, we never saw a cheetah, except for one on a late afternoon.

The sun was getting low and many animals came at this time to drink at the swamp. While watching a lone oryx Local suddenly noticed two cheetah not far from it. However carefully we stalked them, they spotted us long before I could identify them, even through the field-glasses, and raced off into very thick bush. We followed as fast as we could, trying to trace their spoor and at the same time keeping a sharp look-out for elephants, whom we heard rumbling all around us. By then the light was going rapidly and we had to hurry if we wanted to return to the car before dark. On our way we almost ran into an elephant cow dusting herself in a leisurely fashion on the road. A few moments later a whole herd emerged from the bush and joined in the dust-bath. Though it was a lovely sight watching these colossuses blowing sand over each other's wet bodies, which they had obviously just cooled in the swamp, we were most concerned to reach the Land-Rover before being benighted there. Relying on Local's instincts, rather than on mine, to get us out of there we carefully dodged around the elephants until we reached the safety of the car.

A few days later we were once more held up by elephants while driving home after a day-long search. We had found three cheetahs' spoor and very recent droppings on a fallen tree near the Boran boundary, but otherwise no sign of the cubs.

Again it was late afternoon when five elephants blocked the road. I tried the usual tricks to make them move away, such as revving the engine to a roaring sound and shouting. But they went on persistently browsing on a few acacias as though they had all the time in the world for their meal, so there was nothing I could do except turn back and drive round in a long detour. It was dark by the time we reached camp.

At this season many elephants scattered all over the Park but, once the rain started, they would concentrate on areas with sandy soil and thus avoid getting stuck in less porous ground.

Every day we ran into them more often than we cared to. One morning, while following up the fresh spoor of three cheetah, we discovered, not far from Mugwongo Hill, a large limestone deposit. The whole area glittered in the sun from soda crystals concentrated round several springs which oozed from the ground and ran downhill in little trickles. Local lost no time in filling his pockets with these crystals which he valued as much as the many animals who, judging by their spoor, used this place as a salt-lick. We then came upon a most idyllic rocky pool fed by these springs. The water, having passed through a natural filter whilst running underground before trickling into the pool, was clear and most tempting to bathe in. Unfortunately an elephant seemed to have similar ideas as he broke swiftly through the bush to give himself a shower. Quickly we had to give way, and follow the outflow of the pool until it reached a gorge. Its rocky walls were over-shadowed by large trees and creepers, interlaced to form impenetrable curtains, which cut out the heat and glare of the surrounding plains so that I felt as though I had suddenly entered a sacred asylum. But however inviting this cool place was in which to hide from the fierce midday sun, it seemed devoid of life except for the honking of a lone owl who, alarmed by our invasion, broke the weird silence. I looked around the green labyrinth suspecting a leopard of being responsible for the absence of animals but, knowing how well they can conceal themselves, I hardly expected to see one.

As soon as we reached more open ground we saw a herd of about twenty elephants approaching the salt-lick in single file, protecting between them several tiny calves. It was remarkable how the little ones kept up with the quick pace of the adults who seemed in a hurry to reach the water. Knowing how dangerous elephant cows can be when young calves are around, we retreated hurriedly in the opposite direction.

By now the grass fires had started and blazed across the straw-dry plains with terrifying speed. Of course this temporarily upset all animal routines and we had difficulty in retracing the few cheetah spoor which we had followed recently. Two of the most rewarding areas had been the swamps around Mugwongo Hill and the ones close to the Boran border. Since these attracted most of the animals during the present drought, the cheetah also concentrated there. How they might be able to evade other predators, especially the lions who also frequented the swamps for similar reasons, was a constant anxiety for me.

One morning, while driving along the Mulika leading to the lava plateau, we had a puncture. I am not a good mechanic and, defeated by a defective hydraulic jack, I sent Local on foot to the Park's headquarters to get someone to repair it. This meant a great delay in our search as he could not be back in under three hours. Screening the surroundings through my field-glasses during his absence I saw a cheetah, with a cub about four months old, coming from the lava plateau and walking down the ridges to the Mulika. In spite of being at least a mile away they showed up most conspicuously against the recently burned ground. As Local was not there to protect me with his rifle I did not dare to risk walking

cross the wooded plain where we had often encountered
rhino and buffalo. Not being able to identify these cheetah
was particularly frustrating because I suspected the mother
to be Somba, who could by now have had a cub of about this
age had she conceived when we had last seen her ten months
ago. As she had always been fond of this area I was almost
sure that it must be Somba, the more so since her brothers
had been seen on several occasions without her at the swamps
near the Boran border.

When Local returned with the repaired jack we could not
remove the spare tyre as its hinges jammed, and so had no
choice but to drive first to the headquarters to get help before
investigating the two cheetah. Our arrival at the garage coincided with the return of a lorry bringing rangers back from
patrol. They told us of a cheetah with two full-grown cubs
they had seen only ten minutes before and which they could
show us. Hoping that these might be Tatu and her cubs I
decided to give them priority, since the cheetah I guessed
to be Somba would most certainly by now have moved quite
a distance from where I had seen her two hours ago. Guided
by the rangers, we found the spoor of the three cheetah halfway to George's old camp, leading to a little stream. Following the tracks all afternoon we at last caught a glimpse of a
nearly-mature cub running for its life. As by then it was
almost dark we had to postpone our search for Somba to the
next day.

Although we then covered a lot of ground, we only met the
same old rhino which we had got to know so well a year ago,
when Somba and the brothers had shared the area with it.

Naturally we were very happy at having seen at last two
cheetah families which might be Pippa's offspring, though
it complicated our searches considerably since they were in
localities that were at the extreme ends of the Park. From
now on we divided our days between looking around the
swamp near George's camp in the mornings, and the swamps
along the Boran border in the afternoons. This involved many

hours' driving, thus losing a lot of precious time. In order to economize we covered the long distances during the midday heat, when all the animals were likely to be under cover and we could concentrate on spooring. When, after many days, we had not found a trace of either family we centred our efforts on the Boran border. One whole day we walked along both sides of the Bisanadi River, if one could call our struggles through the extremely thick riverbush walking. Creeping, often on all fours, through networks of lianas and thorny scrub we could not see more than a few feet ahead for most of the time, while listening intensely to the slightest sound to give us warning of the buffaloes, whose spoors were everywhere. On one of our attempts to wade through the crocodile-infested river we noticed, only just in time, the eyes of a hippo goggling at us from underneath a palm frond overhanging a pool. It seemed as surprised as we were and, blowing out air with a loud snort, submerged again. Soon after this we nearly collided with a giraffe who had concentrated so much on browsing that she had not been aware of our presence as we stood completely still, watching her. Looking down on us with her soft eyes, she swung her mighty neck around and cantered off.

But however peaceful these animals appeared to be we were horrified to find at almost every drinking-place new or discarded traps and many dried-up branches, evidence of how these traps had been concealed along the animal paths. Local's expert eyes recognized most of these as typical for catching leopard and cheetah, the value of whose pelts the Boran well knew. The thick vegetation belt here was only confined to the river banks, the country immediately beyond was perfect cheetah country, but the animals had to come to this river to drink as it was the only water available in a vast area.

Tormented by the idea that Pippa's cubs might have been beaten to death in a trap (the Boran were known to do this so as not to spoil the skin with spears), I decided to write immediately to the Minister of Tourism and Wildlife begging him to re-open the previously unsuccessful negotiations with the Boran to get this area included in the Meru Park. Under the present arrangement there was hardly any control and not only was poaching made very easy for the Boran but they had also chopped down many raffia-palms, to use the fronds for building huts. Since these palms grew only alongside rivers, the banks would soon be bare of vegetation and the water would dry up if the cutting of the palms went on. I discussed all this later with the Warden, who fully supported me, and hoped my letter might help in saving this valuable area from utter destruction.

A few days later we followed the spoor of a cheetah with a cub, crossing the swamps near the Boran border. They led us to a freshly killed waterbuck fawn which had hardly been touched, and had obviously been abandoned at our approach. We left quickly, hoping the cheetah might return. Soon after this I surprised a serval cat in her midday slumber under a bush. Finding herself cornered she froze, and remained absolutely still until I was within three yards of her and only then ran off. Less courageous were two lionesses whom we found sleeping with three tiny cubs under a tree. As soon as they saw us they sneaked away and settled under a nearby bush, from which they watched us. To my astonishment Local now suggested that we should investigate the cubs which had been left behind. As this would have brought the mother into very fast action, and not in our favour, we retreated instead, step by step, very carefully facing the lionesses all the time until we were out of view.

Half a mile farther on we were led by vultures to a dead kongoni; it was sitting, with its legs tucked under its body and the head resting in front, completely untouched. The vultures had tried hard to penetrate the skin but had not succeeded, although they must have been there for quite a time. Judging from the position of the hartebeest it seemed to have suddenly collapsed, perhaps in consequence of a snakebite.

By now our time here was running short and before leaving

the Park I wanted to go to Elsa's grave. Thanks to our arrangement with the Authorities the area had been kept secret and was, apart from an occasional game patrol, only visited by us. Consequently the access-track had become so overgrown that even I, knowing every inch of it, had difficulty in reaching the place. I found the grave badly damaged; the three euphorbias, which we had planted at its head and foot to symbolize Elsa's cubs, had been uprooted; the cement joints of the cairn had many cracks and the thorn fence around the grave had been destroyed. Judging from the spoor all this was the combined work of rhino, elephant and poachers. Luckily I still had enough cement with me to repair the cracks, while the men replanted the euphorbias and the fence. During the time we were thus engaged I again felt that Elsa was close. Even though I so often think of her, at her camp I always have this strange comforting sensation. Of course my efforts to keep Elsa's and Pippa's graves intact were futile, since both would deteriorate as soon as I was dead. Nevertheless while I was still able to look after them I wanted both to be well kept, even though I realized that it was of far greater importance that Elsa and Pippa should survive not only through their cubs, but also in the hearts of all the millions of people whom they have helped to understand the true nature and character of wild animals. How close I was to having to leave both graves to their fate I only knew the next day.

Early in the morning we met a visitor who told us that he had just seen a cheetah and her cub right on the road. The mother had been especially friendly and had allowed him to take many photographs from within only a few feet of her. He then described the place near the Boran border where we had recently found the spoor of the cheetah and cub who had killed a young waterbuck.

We tracked for several hours, and I was standing on the bonnet of the car screening the bush through the binoculars, while Local concentrated at a short distance on a few indistinct pugmarks, when suddenly he yelled and as he raced back to the car I saw an elephant not more than fifteen yards away, coming straight at us. Instantly I jumped off the bonnet and also dashed into the car, both of us slamming our doors simultaneously. The noise frightened the elephant who was now almost on top of us and, swerving round, under protesting screams, he disappeared. Looking at each other, Local and I burst out laughing, a reaction and anti-climax to our fright. Only now could we appreciate the narrow escape we had had, since we would have had no chance had the elephant not been scared by our doors slamming. I also then realized how badly I had injured by right knee when leaping off the bonnet. Trying to ignore the pain I forced myself to walk, thus hoping to prevent the knee from getting stiff. Perhaps I didn't use the right therapy for it took five months before the knee was right again, despite extensive treatment. Anyway at this time I could not afford to be handicapped, and by sheer willpower continued walking all day, only to see the head of a leopard peeping at us through the grass and vanishing instantly.

Next morning we had better luck in finding the fresh tracks of a cheetah and a cub right on the road within a mile of where the visitor had seen them. They led on to a plain where, after a long search, we lost them. In spite of the oppressive heat we carried on for another hour in the direction we assumed they had taken until, by sheer luck, Local came upon their spoor again. Soon afterwards I spotted a cheetah resting under a tree, unfortunately too far away to identify it even through the binoculars but I assumed it was the mother of the cub. We concealed ourselves as best we could and moved towards it, but the cheetah was gone by the time we drew near. Supposing that it would not move far during the midday heat if we now left it alone, we decided to return at teatime and then approach it from the direction from which it had moved into the area where we had met Whity ten months ago.

My knee was very painful and I could only limp slowly after

Local, who led us, by a long detour which took two hours, back to the spot where I had seen the cheetah. We now found the place alive with elephants, including tiny calves, which not only made our search for the cheetah impossible but needed Local's special bush sense to enable us to dodge safely round the herd. I was desperate. Determined to identify this cheetah, whom I suspected to be Whity, I gave myself an extra day despite the fact that my return to Naivasha was overdue. It seemed unfair that after searching for nearly three weeks, during which we had seen seven cheetah from great distances and had traced many spoor, I might have to depend on the chance photograph of a visitor to identify at least one of Pippa's cubs. I called on this visitor on our way home and he kindly agreed to send me copies of his pictures.

When later I received the photographs I easily identified Whity, who had with her a cub of less than one year old. Both were in excellent condition. It was then plain that it had been Whity whom we had seen under the trees. Judging from the age of her cub it was also obvious that she had kept it concealed from us when we had met ten months ago, and so only now could I fully appreciate her friendly meeting with us then.

To make the best of our last day in the Park we started next morning at crack of dawn. During the night a strong wind must have kindled sparks from the smouldering ground and set most of the plains alight. Nevertheless we safely reached the Boran border swamps, but could not continue to the plain where we had left the cheetah because of thick black smoke spreading over the area. Of course we had no hope of finding them there now as, together with all the other animals, they would scatter for many days before resuming their territories again. Watching the number of birds escaping from the flames and flying, highly alarmed, round us, I thought of the newly born kongoni and waterbuck, impala and Grant fawns, the zebra foals, the ostrich chicks and tiny lion cubs we had observed on our recent searches, and wondered how they would fare in these racing fires.

It is well known that many animals can delay giving birth until the rain produces good grazing for the mothers, who consequently have enough milk for their young. But when nature provided animals with an adjustment to climatic conditions, it did not allow for man-invented grass fires which are ignited at the time that many animals are pregnant. In consequence these fires, along with the many other hazards with which wild animals are threatened, take an additional toll of lives.

Since there was no chance of finding our cheetah here we drove to the Mugwongo swamps, only to find the area equally ablaze. On our way home I saw a cloud of smoke rising in the direction of Pippa's camp, so drove hurriedly there to pack up before all our possessions went up in flames. While we were pulling the tents down the birds dropped from the trees as if expecting titbits. They had never before turned up at midday and I felt very comforted by their friendliness, the more so as I was heartbroken at having to leave without having seen any of Pippa's cubs. Even if I told myself that I had tried my best over all these years to keep them wild, and that if they now reacted in this way I should be happy, they had become so much a part of me that to relinquish them was not easy. But it was a wonderful consolation to know that Tatu and Whity already had their own cubs now and that Mbili, Somba, Big Boy and Tiny were in excellent condition when I had last seen them. I could only pray that the trio might soon have their own families and that all of them would carry on breeding more little Pippas. In that way, Pippa would live on not only in her children – but also in every cheetah for whom she had opened a way to escape life-long captivity.

Nine months passed before I was able to visit Meru again. I arrived on the 16th of July 1971 in the late afternoon at Pippa's camp-site and found Local already waiting for me. He had no news about Pippa's cubs, but told me that he was now in charge of a baby white rhino and that he had been the only person present when the calf was born and ever since had helped the mother to look after it. I knew that for about a year the six white rhino had been roaming free inside the Park and that, when it became obvious that one female was pregnant, a large stockade was built in case she needed protection when her calf was born.

Local said that three months after he and his wife had begun guarding the pregnant rhino, who was in company with another female, he noticed the first sign of labour. They were about three miles from H.Q. at the time. Quickly he sent his wife to collect the Warden, while he warded off the other female who suddenly attacked the pregnant rhino. Lying down she laboured for half-an-hour before the calf was born. Its hind legs came out first. When the Warden arrived, all was over and he could welcome the first female white rhino to be born in Kenya. This happy event crowned the experiment which had started about six years earlier when three pairs of white rhino had been brought from South Africa to Kenya in the hope of rehabilitating them and breeding these rare animals in this country.

Early next morning Local proudly showed me his new charge which had just started to nibble grass. At this early age the little rhino looked even more like a prehistoric creature than the adults do; she was most endearing. I watched her rubbing her fat bottom against a rock, presumably trying to rid herself of ticks, then she followed her mother and the Ranger, who was replacing Local, into the plain and took a leisurely feeding-stroll.

After having taken photographs of the baby rhino Local and I went in search of Pippa's cubs. Following our customary routine he sat on the bonnet of the Land-Rover looking for spoor, while I drove at funereal pace, screening the countryside for cheetah. As soon as Local spotted even the faintest sign of a spoor we followed it up on foot. The last rains had been heavy here and consequently the grass was still high and often made it difficult to see the pugmarks. Nevertheless we persevered day after day, often walking across areas we could not reach by car but where we suspected we might find the cubs. Although we were out from dawn to dusk during the first week we saw only two cheetah hurriedly crossing the road and disappearing into thick bush. Instantly we followed their tracks, creeping for hours through the thorny labyrinth until the fading evening light defeated us. Once, while exploring a rocky river-gorge, Local detected high up in a tree two rhino horns which had obviously been placed there by poachers. The place was only a few hundred yards from one of the main roads where daily carloads of visitors or patrolling rangers passed. Perhaps they surprised the poacher, who hid the horns in the tree and for some unknown reason had not collected his valuable trophy. Local guarded his find jealously until he could hand it over to the Warden for the customary reward.

Knowing now that the poachers were operating right in the centre of the Park I became very worried about Somba, Tiny and Big Boy, whom we had last seen in the Boran country where poaching was also rife.

For several days we concentrated our search along the Bisanadi River but only saw a few python in the water and there was no trace of our cubs. Exhausted after one hot, long morning walk, we rested under the shade of the riverbush for lunch. Local had cut a few fronds of raffia-palm to make a mat for me to lie on while he sat on his own mat, keeping a look-out for any animal which might come for a drink. For some time we had been following the spoor of a lioness with a small cub who must have crossed the river for, from the opposite side, we heard the chatter of vervet monkeys who are usually quiet and only call when alarmed.

Then all was still again, except for the bubbling of the water and the swishing of the palm fronds above us. At last I felt that I was again in my own world and good old Local was part of this world. We knew each other inside out and in the bush were absolute equals, trusting and relying on each other. Lately he had complained that he was getting old and even contemplated retiring soon. He had a smallholding outside the Park boundary where he and his family kept a few goats and grew enough crops to live on. On and off he had lived here all his life and he liked to keep in touch with all that was so dear to him – yet in some way he felt disturbed by the rapid development of the Meru and all the consequences this entailed. During the last days we had been driving along excellent new roads which opened up remote areas and offered splendid views across the Park's magnificent scenery. On my arrival I had seen the Warden in discussion with the architect; they were settling the last details of the new lodge, the building of which was to start next week. Simultaneously new *bandas* to accommodate visitors of simpler tastes were now under construction at Leopard Rock. Besides these, two tented camps were going to be put up, one at the Kenmare site and one farther south along the Tana River. The previous rough river-crossings had been replaced by cement fordings and several camping-sites along the rivers had been cleared to cater for the self-sufficient visitors.

During the years it had taken to develop the Park the wild animals had increased in a marvellous way. For instance I was amazed to see the evasive Lesser Kudu almost everywhere while only a year ago this most exquisite of all the antelopes was only seen on rare occasions and in restricted areas.

When the new lodge would be completed, Meru would undoubtedly become one of the leading Parks of Kenya due to its unrivalled scenic beauty, the great variety of its wild animals and its unique rivers and swamps.

Discussing all these things with Local whom George and I had known for about thirty years, he smiled and in his quiet way remarked: 'All this is very nice of course, but you and I are now the only ones remaining from the good old times, the only "permanenti" here.' I assumed that he referred to Elsa and Pippa which he identified with me and who, for both of us, would be an inseparable part of the Meru Park.

I had been very worried at not finding Pippa's cubs during the last two weeks in which we had driven over 2,000 miles and walked daily up to eight hours through areas which we had selected because they contained the kind of prey cheetah hunt. Also the ground was sandy and this they prefer to high grass where they cannot see lurking predators. At last we were told of two cheetah which had been seen in the early morning close to George's former camp; we were told that the bigger of the two seemed not to be afraid of people though the smaller was very shy. When we arrived at the spot, we found fresh spoor leading into the rocky ground around Mugwongo Hill. We had no choice but to follow the tracks on foot, even though any wild animal will bolt from people walking in the open; they regard a car as harmless. I could only hope that if the friendly cheetah was one of Pippa's cubs it might still remember me, or, should they be wild cheetah, that we could surprise them during their midday sleep and thus identify them before they could run away. Silently we tracked the spoors which soon revealed that both cheetah had been running fast. As I did not want to chase them away from the Mugwongo Swamps, which in the late afternoon were teeming with thirsty animals, we halted our search and resumed it early next morning. After two hours of looking vainly for spoor, I suddenly noticed a cheetah head emerging from the grass under a small bush not far from a swamp. Then a second head popped up but instantly sank back into cover. I drove the Land-Rover very slowly close to the cheetah who was facing us. When I had come within ten yards, a male cub of about fifteen months got up and bolted, growling, while the mother remained immobile. Since no wild cheetah would behave like this, she was obviously one of Pippa's daughters, but which one I would only be able to ascertain if I was able to see the tail-root spots. We looked into each other's eyes for a long time, then the cub returned, wriggling his way through the grass. I recognized him straight away as the same cub whom a visitor had photographed nine months ago together with Whity. The cub was almost a replica of Big Boy and I wondered if he were his son? This was possible since when we last saw them Whity and Big Boy were frequenting the same area near the Boran border. The cub finally settled close to its mother when he saw that she was at ease in our company, but he watched us suspiciously. I took as many photographs as I could before both rolled on to their 'backs and dozed off in the midday heat. When the sun moved and Whity looked for a more shady place, they found it in the shade of a small bush. Now I could clearly identify her by the tail-root spots as Whity. Her son followed but made a detour since we were too near for his liking. After both had settled, I followed with the car which Whity did not mind, indeed she even clasped the cub when he seemed nervous about us. Local and I remained inside the car and only whispered to each other so as not to frighten him: in any case we needed no words to tell each other how happy we were at finding Whity with such a lovely son and both in such excellent condition. Keeping one leg across the other's body, they kept in close contact as they watched out for danger or for prey.

It seemed to me significant that, while the cub looked all around on these alerts, Whity never even glanced in our direction as if she knew that she was safe while we were there. We all spent the hot hours of the day in complete harmony, the cheetah half asleep and we as much relaxed as the heat inside the car permitted – I felt very happy back in my own world. Even if the cultural differences between Local and myself made a close relationship impossible, in moments like these there was no barrier between us and we were both in as much unison with the cheetah as any human could ever hope to be.

As she caressed and licked her son, Whity reminded me very much of Pippa. She was now one month short of five years old, a little older than Pippa had been at the time of her death. Now for three and a half years Whity had lived alone. We had seen her highly pregnant thirty-one months ago (in December 1969). Knowing that Pippa had abandoned her cubs when they were seventeen and a half months old (they could already kill at fourteen months) and having observed that when she left them she was already six weeks pregnant, I calculated that this son of Whity's might well belong to her second litter. Since Whity had been on her own we had seen her twice near Mugwongo Hill and twice in Boran country, as well as once near 'Mile 5'. This area was a triangle of 17 × 12 × 10 km, but since I did not know what routes she had taken to reach these points, nor if she had covered greater distances, I could not ascertain the size of her territory.

By 5 p.m. the heat abated and the cheetah stretched themselves and yawned, then they clasped each other and rolled round for some time. Finally they got up and looked sleepily about them. I was interested to test Whity's memory and so I gave her some water in the tin she had used three and a half years ago. As though it were the most natural thing to do, she came to it and lapped and lapped but her son ran off as soon as I had stepped out of the car. I then made further test of Whity's trust in me by walking slowly up to her and adding Ideal Milk to the water. She just paused from drinking for the time it took me to empty the milk tin and then continued lapping. After I had retreated into the car, the cub sneaked up and tried to get a drink but Whity nipped him in the face whenever he came near the milk, so he sat a few feet away, watching his mother drinking until she had had enough, and walked off. Then he cautiously tasted the milk but did not like it and followed his mother. Chasing and spanking each other, they played for a while, then gambolled out of sight.

Local and I looked at each other. I remarked how wonderfully well Whity had looked after her cub, protecting him from lions and other perils even though she had had no one to teach her about all these dangers. The only explanation was that she had had a perfect mother, whose characteristics had been inherited by her cub. Local listened and after a short silence said: 'This also applies to human beings. If the mother is a good mother, the children will also be good parents.'

Later in the evening I sat beside Pippa's grave reliving the day. Since I had left Meru, one and a half years ago, this was the first time I had again been truly happy. Though Whity and I had lived apart for three and a half years, she still treated me as a friend and had even transferred her confidence in me to her wild cub. Perhaps too, both of them felt my love for them and responded to it? Love was certainly the force which had united us today, the cheetah, Local and myself, even though we all belonged to such different worlds. While thus meditating I saw a red light rising amongst the scintillating stars from the horizon into the dark sky. Could it be a satellite in orbit? Watching it moving steadily higher and higher, I asked myself and had many times before – why do we probe into space where there is no life, while at the same time we destroy life on our planet as rapidly as we can? Evolution has divided our brain, the most highly developed of all creatures, into two parts with conflicting functions: one located in the brainstem, this holds us to an organic life, to our instincts and emotions, which need warmth and love; while the over-specialization of our cortex, in which intellect and spiritual development are centred, separated us from all these basic needs by taking us more and more into spheres where there is no organic life – let alone love. One might regard today's human beings as victims of this schism. We are conscious of the increasing dominance that our intellect is gaining over our instincts, driving us farther and farther from true love and happiness. Why do we not use our dominating cortex to explore the way in which wild animals manage to live in harmony with their environment? Perhaps they could give us the inner peace we can no longer find. Would this not be more useful than reaching for the stars?

Watching the satellite disappearing behind clouds I thought

again of what I had experienced today, and of the years which Elsa and Pippa had allowed me to share their lives. I knew where my world was – it certainly was not in space.

For the next two days we searched in vain for Whity and her son, who evidently had been driven away by the two lions which we found at the swamp, on a kill. Their faces were still blood-smeared from the feast. They moved away, bulging with meat, when I drove near to see what they had eaten. I found only the head of an adult oryx. These antelope weigh up to 400 pounds so, as there was no trace of another predator who might have joined in the meal and vultures had only just arrived, I assumed that each of the lions had eaten half of their prey.

Despite the wonderful reunion with Whity I was worried at not having found Somba, Tiny and Big Boy. By now the eighteen days during which I could remain in Meru were coming to an end. We searched again near the Boran border where I met a Boran who had seen two cheetah several times around this area. After I had given him a generous baksheesh, he showed us the place where he had observed them only two weeks ago. This was not far from where we had parted from the trio nineteen months earlier. We traced the spoor of two under the bush where the Boran had seen them, but as they were a fortnight old, we lost them soon and never found the cubs.

Postscript

I have sometimes been accused of being too emotionally involved in my attitude to animals, and it has been suggested that in consequence my observations will not be regarded as of scientific value; yet, where does a purely scientific, objective study of wild animals lead us to? I have the greatest respect for science, and often regret my lack of academic training, but I have become aware of the danger of losing a general understanding owing to today's tendency to specialize in every field. When doing research on wild animals, the rigid laws and terminology of academic education can not only limit the observer's judgment, and may even lead him to interpret animal behaviour according to the principles he has been taught, rather than allowing him to readjust these principles to what the animals may teach him. I see little value in recording only the outward movements and habits of animals without knowing what motivates them, any more than I think we can judge the actions of persons without knowing the reasons that motivate them.

A purely scientific approach, demanding impersonal, detached, objectively conducted studies, can certainly provide most valuable statistics and general information, but cannot give us deeper insight into the psychology of wild animals which they will only disclose in contact with their own kind. It is, therefore, almost impossible to understand them fully unless one is accepted by them as an equal. This necessitates living with them in close proximity, sharing their moods and problems, and – as a consequence – getting mutually attached. I don't need to say how privileged I feel at having gained the trust, love and willingness to share the lives of the animals which became my great friends. As readers of my books will,

I hope, realize how highly sensitive, emotional and reasoning wild animals can be, they will perhaps agree with me in failing to understand why they should be treated as if they were unable to feel, to love and to think.

We know that we will gain little co-operation between man and man if we apply a purely objective method to research on *Homo sapiens*. Why shouldn't we study animals in such a way, as to learn from them how they contrive procreation, how they communicate, how they establish and respect territories, how they deal with problems we have not ourselves been able to solve?

Why did early man – when he expressed himself in rock engravings and primitive carvings – choose animals as emblems of his aspirations? Why have highly cultured races, like the Egyptians and Assyrians, used animals as symbols for their gods? Why do people today keep pets – even happy families who do not need an escape from emotional starvation – and why are we so deeply moved by tragedies involving our pets? Why are the first toys given to our children representations of animals? Do we need more proof that we need animals more than they need us – that they can give us something which we cannot give ourselves?

The objective scientific method can be an important base for doing research on wild animals. But just as being able to read and write facilitates communication between human beings, neither are ends in themselves and we must never forget that most animals are just as warm-blooded as we are and will only respond if treated with this in mind.

I have come to the conclusion that, provided the observations of an amateur are authentic, a combination of objective and subjective methods yields the best results in research on wild animals. This is especially true if we want to save endangered species from extinction; it is essential that we share their lives, as only then can they show us the way. This was particularly important in Pippa's case. My main interest in sharing her life for four and a half years was to see if I could rehabilitate a tame cheetah to live wild again; to learn why cheetah breed with so much difficulty in captivity, and to find a way of saving these magnificent cats from extinction. Pippa has given us the answer to all these questions, in that she readjusted herself from a thoroughly spoiled pet-existence to a natural life, and bred litter after litter of wildborn cubs because she was able to do this under natural conditions.

My suggestion for saving cheetah from becoming exterminated is to breed them under natural conditions for two generations, to ensure a healthy continuance of the breed, and then to select for their habitat open plains with enough cover for concealment.

In reply to the argument that many endangered species can only be saved by breeding them in zoos, I would like to point out that moving animals from their indigenous habitats to zoos, where they have to adapt themselves to an unnatural existence, only later to be rehabilitated to live wild again, can be a time-consuming and very costly experiment without any guarantee of success. In order to avoid these double readjustments, as well as unnecessary expense, I suggest the transfer of the animals straight into an area where they can live semi-wild until they have adjusted themselves to the new environment, developed immunity against local parasites, and established their territory. Once they have borne young their human helpers should withdraw so that the next generation can grow up absolutely wild and carry on breeding, and thus recover a safe survival population of the species. In order to provide sufficient space for 'breeding threatened species under natural conditions', more protected Game Sanctuaries should have priority in conservation planning.

Appendices and Comparison Table

APPENDIX I

Observation of suckling habits when cubs were one month old
(*see page 23*)

8.45   I arrive. Pippa comes to food-tree, eats ten minutes then returns straight to cubs without a drink. Meanwhile, I find place for sketching and photography. Pippa plays a little with cubs, then off again while I install myself with the cubs spitting at me.
After ten minutes Pippa returns, puts herself into nursing position within four feet of me.

10.15   2 cubs suckle.

10.28   One (female?) stops suckling.

10.35   Second (female?) stops suckling.

All sleep till 11.00: then 2 crawl a little, sleep again until 11.05.

11.13   One (female?) struggles on to Pippa, miaows for milk, pushes nose at teats, but Pippa ignores her. Cub makes soft tremolo, climbs over Pippa to join other cubs; all sleep. Cubs lick Pippa's tongue, their pads, fur.

11.35   One cub suckles till 11.50.

12.05   All wake up, crawl over Pippa.

12.35   3 suckle.

12.40   All suckle till 1.00 p.m., then sleep.

I now give Pippa goat-lung, but she soon goes back to cubs. 1 cub licks paws.

1.30	1 cub suckles, 2 play, 1 sleeps – till 1.45.
1.52	2 suckle.
1.55	4 suckle.
2.05	All sleep away from Pippa near bush centre.
2.30	Wake up, doze.
2.45	2 suckle.
2.50	All suckle.
3.03	All stop. Pippa stretches legs for 2 minutes.
3.35	2 suckle. Female plays with me.
3.40	All suckle.

APPENDIX II

Observation of cubs when they were nine and a half months old
(see page 77)

I spent all day with the cheetah near the 'Photo Tree'. On arrival we meet the family at 'Mile 5', Mulika side; they follow us to 'Photo Tree':

8.30-10.00	Feeding.
10.00-10.20	Cubs play on 'Photo Tree'.
10.20-10.40	Cubs move to small tree 300 yards away. Pippa remains on car.
10.50	I move car more into shade and Pippa hops off. Calls cubs with low voice until she sees them, then all unite and purr. I follow with car to near tree 50 yards.
11.00	One Grant buck and six does within 400-500 yards of cheetah. Pippa alert – the cubs only see Grants few minutes later.
11.05	Pippa stalks the Grants for some 60 yards; sits motionless in hot sun. Cubs are told to stay put?
11.15	Tiny follows Pippa, who stalks on.
11.17	Big Boy and Somba also follow – promptly Grants bolt.
11.20	Pippa gives up and walks to terminalia 100 yards from my car.
11.25	All cubs join her. Grants still in sight but far off. All cheetah sink into grass.
11.31	Big Boy watches for danger, soon joined by Pippa and Somba. Tiny sleeps.
11.35	All sink back into grass. Large plane flies noisily overhead. No response from cheetah.
11.41-11.43	Pippa watches.
11.47-11.49	Pippa, Somba and Big Boy watch.

11.53-11.55	Pippa watches.
12.00-12.02	Pippa watches.
12.10-12.12	Pippa watches.
12.13-12.15	Pippa, Somba and Big Boy watch.
12.18	Pippa comes to car and hops on to roof in shade. I give her water. Cubs follow and rest around car.
12.40	Cubs return to terminalia.
12.44	Pippa hops off and investigates the meat remains inside car.
12.50	Cubs return to car and I give meat remains in front of car, plus water.
1.10	Somba and Big Boy return to terminalia. Tiny and Pippa remain near car.
1.15	Tiny joins other cubs when I sit near him to sketch. I follow soon and sketch dozing cubs; Somba watching me ready to charge.
2.40	Pippa joins us and I sketch on and off until I send Local to look for the spoor of Mbili along Mulika.
4.10	Then I move car to shadier tree; Pippa on roof all the time – cubs around, very sleepy.
5.50	Local returns. Saw several spoor of lions and elephant – but no spoor of Mbili. I still sketch, take photo stills, and leave the still very sleepy family.
6.30	Look for Mbili's spoor along road to Hans Lugga – nil.

APPENDIX III

BREEDING CHEETAHS (*Acinonyx jubatus*) AT WHIP-
SNADE PARK*
V. J. A. MANTON
Curator, Zoological Society of London, Whipsnade Park, Dun-
stable, Bedfordshire, Great Britain.

A two and a half year old female cheetah *Acinonyx jubatus* was
presented to Whipsnade in November 1966. Having completed
six months' quarantine under the Importation of Cats and Dogs
Order she was moved to a grass run where a hand-reared male
called 'Jack' was introduced to her on 3 June 1967. The immediate reaction of the female 'Juanita' was to run from the
male, even to the extent of attempting to climb out of the paddock, round which there was a 2.3 m (7.5 ft) high, 5 cm (2 in)
chain link fence, with a 60 cm (2 ft) angled overhang, giving a
total height of some 2.75 m (9 ft) from the ground. She suffered
one or two skin cuts from the male, but none were serious
enough to warrant surgical interference and the two animals
were left alone as much as possible.

Juanita came into oestrus between 15 and 21 June and a
mating was recorded on 17 June. After this period both animals
appeared to be much more agreeable to each other. No further
signs of oestrus were seen and in August some mammary development was observed. Due consideration was given to moving
the now obviously expectant mother to more suitable quarters
but it was decided to leave her where she was, provide infra-red
heating for the house and a wind-shield for the den and to
remove the male. On 16 September Juanita did not come out
to feed for the second consecutive day and a hole had to be
drilled through the wall of the shed to observe her. She was
seen to be feeding two cubs which appeared healthy and strong.

* Published in the *International Zoo Yearbook*, 1970, Volume 10,
pages 85-86.

Strangely, Juanita did not now appear to resent the presence of humans although she had reacted so strongly to them before. Three cubs were seen with their eyes open five days later. Mother and all three cubs (one male and two female) had to be moved to separate quarters during a long electricity power failure in January 1968. At this time it was noted that one of the female cubs did not appear to be very strong on her hind legs although she had appeared normal during the previous four months in the paddock. X-ray photographs were therefore taken of her legs and these revealed osteodystrophic lesions. She died, following what appeared to be epileptiform convulsions, on 10 February. The other two cubs were transferred to the Hospital where both showed similar lesions. The diet of the adult included whole chicken several times each week but, although red meat was dusted with steamed bone flour before giving it to the cheetahs, it was not possible to observe if the cubs actually ate any such calcium additive.

On 9 April 1968, Juanita and Jack were returned to their original pen and allowed to run together. Again after a short 'scrap' they settled down well and oestrus in the female and service by the male were observed after an interval of ten days. Three more cubs were born on 22 July, although this time the male still had access to the female for at least 24 hours after the birth. He was then removed. Again the cubs proved to be one male and two females. The gestation period was about 95 days whereas on the first occasion it had been 91 days. A closer watch on the diet of the cubs was kept and food was only available to them through a 'creep' so that accurate records were taken of the amounts of food which they consumed. They were taken from the mother on 9 April 1969 in perfect health, and the parents were reintroduced. The 'scrapping' this time consisted solely in the male chasing the female twice round the paddock after which they settled well. Fifteen days later on 24 April, oestrus was again observed and mating recorded.

The paddock in which the parents were kept had a south frontage of 43 m (140 ft) facing on to a public footpath and overlooking the Cape buffalo *Syncerus caffer* and Musk ox *Ovibos moschatus* paddocks. The rear of the paddock was 36 m (120 ft) long and in the eastern half were situated a wooden shed and a kennel. The western boundary measured 15 m (50 ft)

deep and the eastern 21 m (70 ft). Both these were screened
with corrugated iron sheets for a height of 1.2 m (4 ft) from
the ground to prevent the cheetahs from becoming too excited
by the animals kept on either side. The rear fence looks out into
Whipsnade Wood where live peafowl *Pavo cristatus* and North
American turkeys *Meleagris gallopavo* and through which run
Bennett's wallabies *Protemnodon rufogrisea frutica*, Chinese
water deer *Hydropotes inermis* and muntjac *Muntiacus* sp.

The 'kennel' measures 1 m (3 ft) wide and 1.5 m (4.5 ft) deep
and is unprotected from the public on both sides and the rear.
Juanita produced the second litter in here and only moved them
to the shed when the male had been removed. The shed
measured 3 m (9.75 ft) long and was 2.25 m (7.5 ft) deep. It
contained two infra-red lamps, a deep straw bed and the feeding
'creep' for the cubs.

It is interesting to note that on each occasion after the introduction of the male to the female, the initial 'sparring' period
has been followed by a period when both animals remained
closely associated with one another. After mating had taken
place the relationship could only be described as indifferent. In
April 1969 one of the second litter cubs – then about nine
months of age – appeared to be coming into season for the first
time.

APPENDIX IV

FOOD AND SUPPLEMENTS
Daily food-supplements to fresh complete carcasses:
2-4 drops Abidec vitamin
3 teaspoons Farex
1 teaspoon steamed bonemeal
salt
all mixed into diluted Nestlé's Ideal Milk, unsweetened, one-third milk, two-thirds water
1 small tablespoon Calcium Lactate

CHEETAH ILLNESS AND TREATMENTS

Tape Worm: Tenoban tablets, one per 15 lb body weight. To be repeated in two months. *Never* exceed 4 tablets. This drug is dangerous, but most effective.
Yomesan tablets – same dosage.
Dicestol tablets M & B.
Round Worm: Antepan tablets, one per 10 lb body weight. Repeat in two months. Not dangerous.
Ancaris also good; I prefer Antepan.
Distemper (Feline Enteritis): Symptoms: Vomiting.
Hoechst Feline Enteritis Vaccine
Ringers Solution
Glucose injection subcutaneously
Chloramphenical
B-12
Chloromycetin
Iron Dextran
All these are powerful drugs and must be given by a vet.
Babesia Felis (Tick Fever): Symptoms: No appetite, white gums and eyeballs.
Phenamidine subcutaneous injection. Do not overdose.

Arthritis: Butazolidine
Immobilizing Drug: Sernylan (Phencyclidine, Parke-Davis)
Anæsthetic: Sodium Pentathol
Antibiotic Injection: various
Bleeding Gums: Lederkyn tablets
Scaling Pads: Terra Cortril

Medicines given to Pippa while at the Orphanage Hospital between 22nd September and 7th October 1969.

Prednisolon – Cortisone
Glucose
Terramycin
Disinfectant Ointments: Malopan
                         Esophogeal
                         Furacin
Sedatives: Acetylpromazin
            Sernylan
            RO-5-2807

Possible reasons for the decline of Cheetah living under natural conditions:

1 *Leg injuries of cubs between 4-8 months.* This covers the peak of the growing period when the animals need a maximum of minerals. These they get from licking mud, as well as from licking their fur after rolling in sand (calcium).

Cheetah are excellent tree climbers but probably only acquired this habit when they were driven by man from their natural habitat – open plain – and forced into wooded country. Having to make the best of their new environment, they developed rudimentary climbing abilities to enable them to survey their surroundings from trees for prey, and see any lurking danger. Since cheetah are not built for climbing and do not, like other tree-climbing animals, have adhesive pads (like baboon), retractable claws or a low build (like other cats) they frequently injure their long, fragile legs when jumping from heights of twenty feet or over.

2 *Unusually heavy rains* flooding the plains during the first

weeks when cheetah cubs are newly born and the mother cheetah cannot cope with the bad weather conditions without jeopardizing her own health.

3 *Predators* are obviously an additional danger to the survival of young cubs.

Possible reasons why Cheetah do not breed easily in captivity:

Cheetah are very secretive in their habits and carefully conceal their intentions and movements. The fact that life in captivity prevents them from exercising their strong instinct for self-protection may have disturbing effects on their psychology.

They have a great need for exercise, which confinement thwarts (however large the enclosures provided); due to this the female cheetah may be under such emotional stress that she cannot usually breed in these conditions. Exceptions are Krefeld Zoo; Dr Spinelli's Private Zoo, Rome; and Whipsnade Zoo.

COMPARISON TABLE

	Leopard	Lion	Cheetah: 4 litters, 1, II, III, IV
Temperature	101°	100-101°	100-101°
Gestation	90-95 days	105-112 days	90-93 days
Eyes Open	6 days	Probably a few hours after birth. On 3rd day eyes are definitely open. (GEORGE) Only on 5th or 6th day. (CRANDALL)	10-11 days. The clearing of eyes into 3 different shades from dark to light gold took place. II litter 12 weeks. IV litter 14 weeks.
Deciduous Teeth	TAGA: 20 days top incisors start coming through; 22 days bottom incisors through; 24 days all canines through; 34 days lower molars through; 42 days top molars through;	G. SCHALLER: 3 weeks incisors through; 10 days later canines through; 18 days later molars through.	II: 4 weeks top of canines visible. WHITY: 8 months lost both lower canines. MBILI: 8 months lost right lower canines. TATU: 8 months lost both lower canines. IV: 3 weeks 3 bottom incisors and canines through. 2 days later top incisors and top canines through. Molars through at 6 weeks and 4 days (in

	Leopard	Lion	Cheetah: 4 litters, I, II, III, IV
	complete set within 42 days.		cub which was killed by lion). 8 months and 10 days all cubs had lost milk teeth and permanent canines through 2 mm.
Permanent Teeth	In Rhodesia, I saw 2 tame leopards dropping canines at 1 year to make room for permanent teeth.	Canines start at 14 months; with lionesses 6 weeks earlier. (GEORGE) 14-15 months canines came through. (G. SCHALLER)	II litter. (WHITY): 6 months and 1 week 2 molars came through. On 25th of April lower incisors came through. IV: 7 months and 10 days lower canines came through. II: permanent teeth complete at 9 months. IV: 9½ months – bleeding gums, not fully complete set of permanent teeth.
Teats Number of	4	ELSA 5, but only 4 functioned.	PIPPA 13
Markings		To identify: spots along whiskers, and ridge backs, in early youth: spots.	The markings – leading from the eyes across the temples to the neck – are at an early age an almost solid line (similar to the ocelot) which later separates into spots. This also applies to 4-8 spots at the root of the tail which are often con-

	Leopard	Lion	Cheetah: 4 *litters*, I, II, III, IV
			nected in young cubs and always keep solidified. I found these solidified tail spots to be the most reliable way to identify cheetah. The spots across the flanks of very young cubs follow distinct lines from the spine to the belly. (Are these early markings like those of the now extinct King Cheetah?)
Baby Fluff	On back and neck lost yellow fluff at 4 weeks.	4-6 weeks woolly coat changes to sleek one.	13-14 weeks loose fluffy grey hair remains only on the shoulders.
Length *Average*	7 feet 5 inches	9 feet lion 8 feet lioness	PIPPA: 7 feet 4 inches; of this the tail accounts for 2 feet. Male much larger.

HABITS

		Lion	Cheetah
Birth		ELSA concealed her 3 cubs for 6 weeks before bringing them into camp to us.	PIPPA guided me to her cubs when I litter 10 days old (3 cubs born 14.3.1966, killed by predator before 6 weeks old). II litter 5 days old (3 females, 1 male, born 19.8.1966).

	Leopard	*Lion*	*Cheetah:* 4 *litters,* I, II, III, IV
			III litter 8 days old (4 cubs born 28.3.1968, killed by predator on 9th April).
			IV litter 10 days old (3 males, 1 female, born 15.7.1968).
			SECOND GENERATION: WHITY, female of II litter, was seen with a cub about 1 year old on 19.10. 1970. (WHITY was then 4 years and 2 months).
			TATU, of II litter, was seen with 2 almost fully grown cubs on 21.7.1970. (TATU was then 4 years less one month.)
Moves Cubs		Within a week.	PIPPA moved II & III litters 1st time before eyes opened at 11 days.
			IV litter 1st time at 16 days.
			II litter 21 moves in 6 weeks.
			IV litter 14 moves in 6 weeks.
Movement	TAGA: At 2 weeks could walk clumsily. At	At 4 weeks could walk	At 10 days could crawl.
			At 3 weeks walked steadily.

	Leopard	Lion	Cheetah: 4 litters, I, II, III, IV
	4 weeks walked fast and could climb up a chair or the wire of her enclosure.		
Start Eating Meat	TAGA: At 6 weeks less 1 day.	At 8 weeks. Have milk and meat until 4 months.	II and IV litters: 5 weeks.
Lap Water from Bowl			II litter 5 weeks and half. IV litter 6 weeks and 3 days.
Stop Drinking Milk	At 3 months (PETER TURNBULL KEMP)	At 8 months	II: At 8 weeks last seen to suckle At 14 weeks Pippa's teats are dry. IV: At 11 weeks and 5 days Big Boy last seen suckling. At 5 months and 18 days (24 weeks and 3 days) Pippa's teats are dry. (I squeezed them almost daily.)
Eating Habits	Hold meat in position with paws.	Hold meat in position with paws.	Tear or gnaw meat off while keeping front legs bent up to shoulder.
Cover Food with Earth	Yes.	Yes.	Yes, but only when eating a complete carcass or kill; never

	Leopard	Lion	Cheetah: 4 *litters*, I, II, III, IV when I brought cut up meat.
*Eating Mud**	Yes.		Yes.
Eating Grass		Yes.	Yes.
Like Swimming	No.	Yes.	No.
Sound	Wa-wa indicates comfort, high-pitched miaow expresses distress; cough	Well known and described in Elsa books.	Comfort – purr, wa-wa, nyam-nyam; command when at ease – prr prr prr; when worried calling cubs – I-hn I-hn very low volume: II at 3 weeks first chirp. IV at 17 days first high-pitched chirp; at 6 weeks and 3 days first prr prr; at 9 weeks and 3 days BIG BOY made new flute-like high-pitched sound while watching us suspiciously. TINY made new squealing sound within 17 months when intimidating SOMBA. Preceding mating, a sharp rattling long prrrr prrrrr.

---

* Mud, I assume, contains ground limestone essential for providing animals with sufficient calcium.

	Leopard	Lion	Cheetah: 4 litters, 1, II, III, IV
Come into Season Before Ready to Mate		2-2½ years, lionesses.	PIPPA started her own long safaris at 15 months together with a male. MBILI did the same at 16 months, was away for 17 days.
Mating Starts		ELSA: 3 years GIRL: 2 years and 8 months. SUKI: 3 years and 2 months.	PIPPA: 2 years, conceived. IV: 16½ months.
Prey		From eland to dik-dik, buffalo, giraffe, etc.	Duiker, small Grant, young waterbuck, dik-dik, any antelope fawn, yellow-neck (francolin) guinea-fowl, pigeon, young ostrich.
First Kill	Less than one year (PETER TURNBULL KEMP)	ELSA's cubs left to fend for themselves at 14 months. Normal: 17-18 months.	II WHITY: 14 months (possibly earlier) killed a duiker near my camp. IV: 11 months assisting mother in killing. 14 months kill independently of Pippa.
Cubs Become Independent of the Mother	1 year to 18 months (PETER TURNBULL KEMP)	2 years.	After II cubs were 15½ months old, PIPPA started leaving them alone ½ day and more later. At 16 months MBILI away

	Leopard	Lion	Cheetah: 4 litters, I, II, III, IV
			for 17 days. At 17½ months PIPPA abandons II litter. At 18 months PIPPA looks for new nursery for III litter near camp, since she had mated when II litter were 16 months old. IV litter: BIG BOY keeps within 8½ months away from family for a few hours. At 11 months cubs separate from mother for the day at distances of ¼ mile. When cubs 14 months PIPPA has accident and from then onwards cubs live entirely on their own.
Oestrus		Every 4-5 weeks. GIRL lost her first 2 cubs at 2 months and mated again immediately.	PIPPA lost her I litter at about 6 weeks old, and mated again within 3 weeks. Conceived. When III litter was killed, at 13 days, she mated within a week. Conceived.
Social Instinct	Solitary.	Gregarious.	Solitary – except for the 18 months the cubs remain with the mother.

	Leopard	Lion	Cheetah: 4 litters, I, II, III, IV
Claws Re-tractable	Yes.	Yes.	No. (Sketch attached.)
Litter Size	1-5	1-5	1-6
Age		15-18 years.	14 years.
Territorial Demar-cation		Male and female.	Male and female.
Scent mark-ing: Defecation on elevated locations; trees, ant-hills, etc.			Male and female.
Climb Trees	Yes.	Yes.	Yes.
Nocturnal	Yes.	Yes.	Yes, but mainly males only.
Diurnal Mating		Yes.	Yes.
Final Neck Bite of Male to Female		Yes.	Yes.
Carrion Eater	Yes.	Yes.	No.
Illness	TAGA died of *Babesia felis*	ELSA died of *Babesia felis*	PIPPA was cured of *Babesia canis*. DUME died of *Distemper felis*

This list is based on my own observations except where another source is quoted; i.e. my husband George, G. Schaller and Peter Turnbull Kemp.

CAT CLAWS

When not in use, the claw-bearing joint of each toe is folded back over the preceding joint and held in place by a ligament. In this position it is encased in a sheath of skin for further protection. When the animal extends its paw to strike, a tendon attached to each toe, pulls the joint forward and bares the claws for instant use. The cheetah differs from other cats in the absence of claw sheaths. The blunt claws always remain extended and exposed.

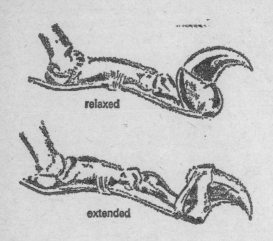

relaxed

extended

THE ELSA WILD ANIMAL APPEAL

This appeal was launched by Joy Adamson to help solve the many problems connected with the conservation of wild life in Africa today. It is registered as a charity in the United Kingdom and Canada and donations may be sent to:

The Elsa Wild Animal Appeal
c/o The Charities Aid Fund
48 Pembury Road
Tonbridge
Kent

The Elsa Wild Animal Appeal of Canada
P.O. Box 864, Postal Station K
Toronto 12
Ontario
Canada

Fontana Books

Fontana is best known as one of the leading paperback publishers of popular fiction and non-fiction. It also includes an outstanding, and expanding section of books on history, natural history, religion and social sciences.

Most of the fiction authors need no introduction. They include Agatha Christie, Hammond Innes, Alistair MacLean, Catherine Gaskin, Victoria Holt and Lucy Walker. Desmond Bagley and Maureen Peters are among the relative newcomers.

The non-fiction list features a superb collection of animal books by such favourites as Gerald Durrell and Joy Adamson.

All Fontana books are available at your bookshop or news-agent; or can be ordered direct. Just fill in the form below and list the titles you want.

FONTANA BOOKS, Cash Sales Department, P.O. Box 4, Godalming, Surrey. Please send purchase price plus 5p postage per book by cheque, postal or money order. No currency.

NAME (Block letters)

ADDRESS